Life at the Crossroads
Reflections from a Country Store

Robert Felde

ISBN: 1-4392-3956-8
ISBN-13: 9781439239568

To order additional copies, please contact us.
BookSurge
www.booksurge.com
1-866-308-6235
orders@booksurge.com

Table of Contents

Readers respond to *Life at the Crossroads*

- *An outstanding job of bringing back the simpler days; before mass market stores and a convenience store on every corner. This book will enlighten those who have never seen a real country store and bring back pleasant memories for those who shopped in one. The author's description of the country store is so vivid that the reader becomes a part of the store.* IA

- *Broader than one community, it represents the life of a bygone era that people can relate to in their own communities across America.* MN

- *A delightful book that readers of all ages will appreciate. Felde describes the environment of his youth in such a way that one can't help but become attached to the country store and the cast of characters that frequently assembled there…captures the essence of rural life with honesty and humor; and the memories that he shares are as heartwarming as they are engaging.* Decorah (IA) Public Library

- *The chapter on tobacco was so descriptive I felt myself back on the planter and in the barn stripping tobacco after "case" weather.* IL

- *Both my book clubs have selected this book to read.* IA

- *What an amazing book! So many memories, in such an eloquent way.* WI

- *It was so well written; I laughed and cried...certainly achieved the goal of reflection and touching people's hearts.* WI
- *Intelligent, perceptive, well written.* IA
- *Focusing on the store and the role it played...as both observer and participant, the author succeeded in giving the reader an understanding of family and working life, with skill, humor and insight.* CT

Acknowledgements

There are many people from the West Prairie community (and those who happened to traverse our crossroads) who deserve a thank you, both for their lives that drove the stories and accounts in this book and, more importantly, were part of the contributing village of my childhood. Many are named in the book, and others are unnamed but part of the bigger community picture. To attempt naming them all would result in unfortunate omissions. Regretfully, many are now gone and unable to share again in the stories that shaped my life and the community in which we lived.

I always thought I grew up in an unusual situation, somewhat embarrassed and perhaps even felt sorry for myself for living in a slightly run-down country store. That immature judgment of youth gave way to an appreciation for my parents, aunts, and uncles, who guided me with love and support through an environment ripe with learning opportunities and rich community legacies.

My wife, Marty, has been very supportive. She knows that writing is good for the soul and that stories are important. And she was careful to critique only to the extent that I could tolerate. My children thought it was cool that I was writing a book and I thank them for that encouragement.

Numerous friends and colleagues have provided me with opportunities to think about mentoring and how it influences the lives of young people, and allowed for reflective writing opportunities to share the impact of mentors in my life. Thank you to those people.

And finally, I appreciate the rich work by Ben Logan in *The Land Remembers*. His account of a slightly earlier farming generation, very near West Prairie, stimulated my interest in recording stories that are too easily lost in a busy world that desperately needs reflection.

Chapter 1
Crossroads

The West Prairie Store, at the crossroads of Wisconsin State Highway 82 and Vernon County Trunk N was my childhood home. It was also called the Allen Halverson Store, after my grandfather who built and opened the store in 1894. To friends and neighbors, it was affectionately known simply as "the store." And I actually lived there, in the penthouse apartment above the store with my parents, Helen and Lee, and an older brother Dave. It may sound romantic to say that I lived in a penthouse apartment when I was growing up, but the reality was far from it. And the word itself, penthouse, was really a big city term that may have been jokingly applied once to our residence, in passing, by one of the few country folk who would have known what a penthouse was. I doubt that anyone really even called our residence an apartment. To most folks we just lived at, or above, "the store."

I choose to tell the story of growing up at the crossroads because it is an important story of life in community, and the story of a rich era in rural America that has mostly faded away.

Stories are what we remember and the manner in which we share our perception of reality – how we recount the truth and deeper meaning of what has transpired.

Sometimes we don't understand that story until years later, when we have reflected on the happenings and metaphors in our lives, like living at the crossroads. A perfectly accurate account of what happens is only bare history, and I make no pretence that all my accounts are historically perfect. But perhaps the blended recollections serve to gather the richness of the story.

The story itself wanders in and out of the store, its proprietors, the community and social influences during the early 1950's, the earliest memories of my childhood, to the late 1960's when I left the community and ventured off to college.

There were two golden ages for the store, one before 1950 and another that, with bias, I perceive and define as the Golden Age of the Coffee Table. By 1950 the past glory of the West Prairie Store had begun to fade. From its origins prior to 1900 until the 50's there were many transitions and rich stories. From transportation by horse and buggy to modern automobiles, the store had sold all the accouterments of travel, including Titan tractors and Overland automobiles. Stories are told of huge ice chunks harvested from the Mississippi River and stored in the ice house where they lasted well into the summer. Eggs and chickens were shipped to Chicago after they had been bartered for other groceries. Dry goods and farm supplies made the store at the crossroads a full service community center. Farm implements were sold and the business was enhanced by a blacksmith shop in an adjacent building. An open field across the road would host traveling gospel tents, and cautious clerks would monitor bands of gypsies as they traversed the prairie. For forty years, the store was a United States Post Office, until the final stamp was cancelled in 1935.

But as the post World War II era arrived, changes were evident. There was an acceleration of transportation modes. Rural schools, though still healthy community centers, could foresee a future of consolidation. Once a center for virtually all the rural needs, the store found its identity slowly changing along with the landscape of rural America. Larger farms and more sophisticated machinery emerged. Families became smaller, and children were more inclined to leave the farmstead. Once a landmark that was unquestionably the center of commerce and community (since there was no other option) the store slowly and unconsciously transitioned into another era.

The store founder, Allen Halverson, died in 1947, and his wife Bertha in 1955. Store proprietorship fell to the two children who were still living at home; I affectionately call them Uncle Alfred and Aunt Ruth. They remained single and lived in the family farmhouse just to the west across County Trunk N, where Alfred also maintained an 80 acre family dairy farm. The penthouse above the store had housed a variety of tenants since the early years when Allen and Bertha and their youngest children lived there. But in 1947, the youngest of their daughters, Helen, and her husband Lee, moved into the penthouse to assist in store operations as well as purchase an additional 80 acres of adjacent farm land. They were my parents and my life at the crossroads began in 1950.

What I recall and shape into stories of the next two decades is selective. Since much of my life was literally in the store, the accounts of my parents and brother may seem slighted. That is merely a function of place. Their influences were strong and spiritual and shaped my life in multiple ways, but much of that is another story. My brother's birth order shaped us both. He was four years my senior, and as such, migrated quickly into the ways of the farm. Almost by default I was less mechanical, an errand runner, and a natural orphan to the wonders of the country store that sat below our penthouse.

Included in my memories of the community, culture and coffee table tales, are a few scandals, harshly spoken words, and tragedies of relationships. There would be nothing positive in recounting the details of those except in tangent reference to how a community shares and moves on. There was never anything perfectly idyllic about the community at the crossroads and I don't wish to portray such a picture; the intent is to simply illuminate what a community might be, either decades ago or in a new world of crossroads that we all traverse.

Aunt Ruth and Uncle Alfred

Chapter 2
Coffee

"We would have made more money if we had sold the coffee and given away the groceries." That was my father's reflection in the latter years as he recounted what the store life had really been like. He was right, particularly if it had been priced like some of the trendy coffee shops of today; shops that are neat and tidy, geared for people to grab and run, or isolate themselves behind a table only large enough to allow them to prop up the daily paper as shelter from the neighbors around them. Drinking coffee at the store wasn't trendy, neither was it grab and go—it was the basic social fabric of West Prairie community life.

It was during my early childhood when Alex, a grandfatherly neighbor significantly skilled in carpentry, enlarged a counter in the back of the store into a table top, made from composite wood and finished in dark brown tones that would eventually absorb and mask any coffee stain presented. The edge of the counter top table, which now protruded nine inches beyond the original counter top and drawers, was skillfully lined with a metal ring that withstood years of the toughest of leaning, grabbing and scraping by its guests and their children. And to the south of the coffee table was the back wall of the store where Alex's cabinetry handiwork had enclosed a sink, drying rack and cupboard in a golden yellow finish, so that the rear of the store now had the feel of a small kitchen, surrounded by other counters, glass cabinets, a large iron safe, roll top desk, and meat slicer. A rotating menagerie of rickety kitchen stools surrounded the counter. To complete the homelike feel, a television with rabbit ears perched on the safe, easily visible from most of the coffee table.

Although I was not there to remember what the store was like in previous years, this was undoubtedly the Golden Age of the Coffee Table. During this era came the transition from an electric coffee pot (or two, at some times) that could percolate 8-10 cups, to the coffee maker that could handle 30 cups per round of service. Various renditions of wall plaques surfaced (donated by patrons) with phrases that reminded all who gathered that there was something special about fellowshipping around coffee, and one even clearly distinguished those who gathered there as being privileged members of the "West Prairie Coffee Drinkers."

At this time of era transition in the store coffee itself, as a product, was changing. Although the commercial coffee grinder in the backroom of the store was still there, it had become a thing of the past. The fresh ground coffee had given way to metal cans of Butternut, Hills Brothers, and Nustad's coffee. While there were rarely multiple brands of anything on the store shelves, three coffee labels suggested the prominence and significance of that product to the store and community. Unfortunately the Nustad brand, with its artistic yellow mustard colored can and the brown "Hound Dog Pointer," was the first victim of shelf competition. The green coffee grinder remained on a backroom counter shelf not far from the black cylinder and electric bulb contraption that had been used to check eggs for live embryos before they were sold. (The egg was placed against a slightly smaller than egg size hole in the cylinder and became virtually transparent.) These and other throwbacks to days of local bartering and bulk product sales, along with the old crank style phone gradually disappeared from the store property, finding their way to friends and opportunists who saw their decorative or antique value. They missed absconding with the valuable World War II vintage Coca-Cola posters, mostly because they were nailed to the wall behind storage shelves.

There was a certain rhythm and flow that defined life in the store, most of which centered around the coffee table. It began every morning between 6:30 and 7 a.m. Usually it was Uncle Alfred who was there to make the coffee and open the doors for the bread man, the first visitor of the day. Butch was always there with his large box shaped yellow and blue Sunbeam Bread truck, ready to stock the white metal rack, just inside the front door, with a variety of breads and cakes. And he was the cornerstone of the first round of coffee drinkers that included the early rising retired farmers and tradesmen who didn't need to be in the barn milking cows at this early hour. Philosophical and political conversations, usually of the conservative bent, supplemented the usual discussion of local news, weather, and crops. Earl was always a stable presence because his profession as a plumber and well repairman allowed personal control of his time, and he could always report on the shore fishing scene at Victory, ten miles away on the Mississippi, or the latest walleye happenings on the fishing barge below the dam at Genoa. The early gathering was the most likely group to venture into the "100,000 miles on my car conversation" and trips to the vehicle were appropriate to confirm this milestone. (Such a milestone also suggested retirement or enough success to afford travel time, since most farmers were locked into milking cows, morning and night, seven days a week.) Although there was never inhospitable behavior, Earl was deftly ready with a sly comment if a farmer ventured in for early coffee before he had been to the barn for morning milking; it was clearly a social faux pas, as well as a negative reflection of his farming habits. Earl was also ready to advise any intruder, in no uncertain terms, if they had inadvertently settled into his self proclaimed reserved seating at the table.

The coffee table was mostly just a setting for coffee in the early mornings, but the bread man would occasionally open a package of donuts or Danish rolls. The adventurous soul might have joined Alfred in breakfast, particularly if it was one of his "thirty things you can do to Malto-Meal" efforts. His cooking forays were limited, but periodically he would engage in creative cooking binges that produced such delicacies as pickled watermelon. It was easier to humor him on the breakfast menu.

Whether it was over breakfast or simply coffee, weather fueled almost every conversation in a farming community; and so it also fueled the morning humor. And rain provided a more relaxed atmosphere amongst the coffee crowd. When Chester recorded 1.75 inches of rain from the night before, and Herman strongly protested the measurement since his gauge recorded something distinctly different, it was Earl who slipped out of the store and filled their gauges to equal, but even higher, levels. Of course upon his return he was happy to report back to them that he had recorded a different level (that coincided with their new levels) on his own instrument, and perhaps they had best do another reading to make sure they had been correct.

It is hard to pinpoint how they figured out the ruse later on in the morning, but it was accompanied by Chester's typical, "Well, I didn't think that seemed right," Earl's deep raspy laugh that suggested but never admitted responsibility, and Herman's chuckle and expressive "By Jinx!" This was accentuated by a swelling up in his cheeks that might have predicted a forceful ejection of tobacco chew (fortunately we never accommodated customers with spittoons), but the only outcome was a short tweet that suggested he was spitting a gnat from between his lips.

But Earl was also the occasional recipient of the gag, including Uncle Alfred's substitution of a plastic look-alike into Earl's regular stash of sugar cubes on the coffee table. (There was no better treat for a kid at the coffee table than one or two well soaked sugar cubes – it satisfied the sweet tooth, and allowed a palatable excursion into the adult experience of coffee drinking.) Earl never admitted whether he ate the cube, or quietly picked up on the trickery and slipped it into his pocket. But as usual, he delighted in holding the secret trump card, laughing at my father's report to him that Alfred had obsessed for days over concern that the plastic might have done him some harm.

A second round of drinkers ventured in between 8:30 and 9:30 a.m., and included a more random and irregular mix of farmers who had completed their first round of morning chores and were looking for a break and maybe some farm supplies. But this crew which was less disposed to long conversations, would often say, "Just half a cup." They knew that the day was still young and work was waiting. This time frame also presented the first quick visits of those who might have been classified as the young farmer soda pop drinkers. The convenience store existed in the country long before the cities, and we sold sodas, donuts, chips and candy for those on the run. Maybe some rain or heavy dew would allow them an extra sip or two of coffee, or some conversation, before they ventured off to rake or bale hay.

The first two groups usually limited their shopping to sodas and treats, gasoline, a few loaves of bread, coffee, chewing tobacco, cigarettes, or some farming essentials such as gloves, baling twine, or salt blocks. The third round of coffee drinkers, women of the community who might be there for actual grocery shopping, rarely felt safe before 9:30 a.m. By then Aunt Ruth had made her appearance in the store, after early morning hours of gardening, baking pies, or doing other household chores in the family home just across County Highway N. Plans were concocted for the next church dinner, the upcoming Secret Pals gathering, or what the program would be for the next Ladies Aid at the church. Health concerns and hospitalizations were reviewed, as well as the latest in school news, and recipes (particularly experimental ones that had found their way to the store coffee table).

Departure of the women's group was gradual, but clearly finalized if someone (most likely neighbor Bernice) commented that it was just about time for the mailman to arrive and that she had better get home to prepare lunch. So by late morning the coffee table scene began unfolding for another meal, but not necessarily for the proprietors. We didn't sell lunch; however, we provided a simple lunch, free of charge on daily basis to the mailman, and occasionally to salesmen or friends whose timing and open schedules coincided with that of postal deliveries. The first lull in coffee drinking began during this lunch hour when most folks were at their homes. Assorted delivery men worked their way through the noon hour and usually lunch was rushed, eaten standing up, almost always in shifts for Aunt Ruth and

Uncle Alfred. Once the electric frying pan had become a staple part of the coffee table corner, meals took on a hit and run approach. But at least they could be warm; whether it was a casserole (hot-dish in local vernacular), or a long simmering meat offering that was supplemented by a can of the vegetable du jour, that went straight from the shelf to the aluminum pan on the hot plate next to the electric fry pan. Almost any meat could be dressed up with some variety of Campbell's Soup for long and tender cooking.

There was a solitary, almost sacred, time that emerged some days in the early afternoon. It was really too early for afternoon coffee for most folks, at least not to gather as a group. Nobody ever really said it, but if one looked closely, they might have observed that this was the time when the solo coffee drinkers found their way to the store. It may have been the less social of the farmers' wives, or it may have been the woman who was avoiding the social grouping and needed this distinct, isolated time to pour out her sorrows and tears along with a cup of coffee. Some consolation, the comfort of a bible verse, and many unanswered questions rested at the table at this time of day. It would be easy to jokingly call the store a non-profit social service agency, but it wouldn't have been a joke. There never was significant financial profit during those years, and the coffee table was, in reality, a rural counseling service that catered to the disappointments and lost opportunities of the farm wives or the stoic sadness of a lonely farmer. And the coffee table did that, mostly because it provided what we instinctively know is good counseling – an open door, a non-threatening invitation, and space at the time when it is needed.

The other potential coffee drinker in the early afternoon was the preacher's wife. While the role of the pastor's spouse was beginning to transition during this era, the careful wife was sensitive not to create the impression of being a social gadfly about the community or be too much involved in the regular gatherings, so this time slot was safe for her also. Of course there was the unwritten code that what was said quietly in the company of one at the coffee table, was something that remained there. We went the extra mile for her by constructing a stile across the orchard fence so she could leave the adjacent parsonage door, traverse through the orchard and back yard of the "big house" (an affectionate term for Halverson family farmhouse that Aunt and Uncle lived in), and approach the store without being frequently seen on the highly traveled thoroughfare of State Highway 82.

Late afternoon was a conglomeration of folks, not as defined in groupings as perhaps earlier in the day. Many were in the good friends category, and frequently they were there for the second trip of the day. Leftover cookies and bars were served, or supplemented by new offerings from the visitors. The crowd depended upon the time of year and the flow of farm work. During the school year the group included my mother, and others—sort of hanging out and waiting for the school bus to arrive. The phone would sometimes ring with a young caller just off the school bus attempting to locate his or her mother. And if mother wasn't there, it was a good bet that someone in the store would know where to find her. It was a good time to unwind after the day's labor and see neighbors, but an especially good time to catch up on school news or the dating scene in high school, how a sports team was doing, or who had made the cheerleading squad. And, of course, there was a bit of gossip.

The spiciest gossip was that of teenage pregnancy. But then again, if it was true, it was more like news than gossip. One memorable afternoon when the coffee group was surprised that a local girl found herself in "the family way," someone uncharacteristically offered, "I didn't know she had it in her." The possibly off-color double entendre retort that followed from a high school senior precariously danced the fine lines of word choice that would give adults pause, but not quite allow them to pass judgment regarding intent. Such conversations by younger members of the community in the afternoon gathering provided a gradual, local rite of passage and transition into the adult farming community.

Other sporadic guests could arrive anytime, but especially in the summer travel months, such as the richer relatives from California, who beckoned us to do the obligatory visiting in their white air-conditioned Cadillac that they parked beside the store. While it was a spacious car, not everyone fit in, so I mostly managed curious glances and waves from outside the parlor on wheels. I never fully sorted out the reasons for this hit-and-run visit—whether it was the severe summer heat, a legitimate health concern that necessitated an air-conditioned environment, or if it might have been a slight disdain for the humble store environs, including the unpredictable interactions with locals who never hesitated to join in conversation.

Extra special guests would unpredictably grace our presence at the coffee table. One such person was Mary, a young local woman and preacher's daughter, who left for college and eventually moved off to a new world and marriage. But she persisted in her coffee table visits with Aunt Ruth and my mother, seeking their stable and caring interest, even as she transitioned away. That is not to say that it was a one way relationship; she brought a spark and freshness of youth to her respected elders when she returned to the prairie. And in those visits, she was always solicitous of my presence as a young admiring kid willing to soak up stories of college and the outside world. On one of her visits she gave me a small, carved wooden frog. I am not sure the present had any particular significance, except that it was given to me; and it remained a valued possession for many years. Eventually, my path crossed with Mary's daughter years later. Illness had claimed Mary's life before her daughter could experience the fullness of her caring mentorship. I gave her the frog, hoping it would provide a comforting memory. She still has the frog; it retains its coffee color and silently, gently, holds stories of hope from the coffee table.

The regulars knew that any coffee remaining in the pot after 5 p.m. was too strong, and asserted that those who hadn't made it to the store earlier in the day deserved what they got.

***

There was another store life in the evening. Technically we closed at 6 p.m. on Monday, Wednesday, and Friday and remained open until 9 p.m. on Tuesday, Thursday and Saturday. The hours were artificial since Ruth and Alfred lived in the store more than they lived in the spacious farmhouse across the road. Maybe Ruth would eat breakfast before coming to the store, but the house was large and lonely, and the store held more appeal than simply being a convenient food source.

Supper might happen whenever patrons started to clear, either because of closing hours or simply the diminished business around chore time in the evening for the farm families. I would often gravitate to the store for supper, particularly in the summer when school activities didn't occupy my time. My favorite dinner with Uncle Alfred was ring bologna, specifically Farley's bologna from the popular LaCrosse vendor whose deep red refrigerated truck would delivery wieners and luncheon meats on a weekly basis. The bologna was best when boiled, cut in thin slices and folded into a generously buttered white bread sandwich, sometimes dripping the freshly melted butter to an unprotected sleeve or countertop.

On a night when the store was closed, supper might involve a neighbor or two sharing a special offering like oyster stew. The front lights of the store would be shut off, and maybe even the front door locked, but occasionally folks would still stop in, having seen the dim lights in the back of the store, and perhaps the television flickering its black and white images. These customers would politely inquire about the store being open, and the response never conveyed that we were unequivocally closed, only that, yes, we were closed, but were nevertheless happy to get them something. Favorite television shows such as *I Love Lucy*, a perennial favorite that provided a wacky relief for Aunt Ruth and friends, often accompanied the suppers.

The store hours were even more artificial on the nights that we were "open." Generally it fell to Uncle Alfred to tend the store on those evenings. The evening crowd gathered with no cookies, treats or even coffee; and had shifted from the coffee table to a horseshoe configuration of benches and wooden chairs that surrounded the bread rack, directly inside the front door. Some would sit on the large wooden counter that divided the overall, boot and glove shelves of the western wall from the store aisle. And the crowd was different also – all men including the Norwegian bachelor farmers, and the young married farmers seeking a bit of conversation and fellowship after the evening chores. Freshly shaved farmers with clean overalls and a hint of aftershave were always appreciated, but not necessarily the norm. Evenings in the store often displayed new overalls that had not yet hit the barnyard scene, reserved for trips to town or lesser social gatherings, crisp and fresh. Preferably they were blue/grey and white striped Big Smith brand, suggesting they had been purchased in the store. We tolerated the plain dark blue denim of Key or some other brand, or even the rare pair of plain blue jeans (most farmers opted for overalls instead of jeans, since the overalls prevented hay from slipping in and scratching parts unknown) but wondered about the store of origin. Often a blue haze of cigarette smoke smothered the room, mingling and slightly masking the smell of manure that may have remained on rubber boots or work shoes. Sales were limited to ice cream treats, soda pop and nicotine stimulants.

Alfred ultimately realized that sitting in the store on a hot summer night was boring, as well as hot, so he and others constructed two lighted horseshoe courts just to the east of the store. It was an easily accomplished task with his electrical background, and the support of friends who could readily dig holes for the light poles and construct the necessary pits. It never cost us any business, since there was really none to lose, and may have even resulted in a few extra soda pop sales to new "customers" who were drawn into the social and recreational aspects of horseshoes. Most of the time the store itself remained unattended and it was a serious inconvenience if we had to leave the social network of the horseshoe court and tend to a customer.

Saturday night was an extension of the other open nights, except that the conversations went on longer, the political discussions were more intense, and the urgency of another day of work lessened with Sunday and its respite only a few hours away. Alfred was always there. Johnnie, puffing on his pipe, might have regaled the crowd with his accounts of crawling on hands and knees to approach a secret trout hole somewhere in the Bristow valley only a few miles away. Someone shared how soybeans were grown in the neighboring state of Iowa and how they might replace many corn acres in southwest Wisconsin. And maybe the local social services office was roasted with commentaries about their subsidies to undeserving slackers.

Something in my value system—perhaps fueled by my parents, whose bedroom was directly above the front of the store and who indirectly and unwillingly participated in the marathon Saturday night sessions—told me this late night crowd was intruding and taking advantage of an exhausted uncle lacking the assertiveness to shuffle off the visitors and close the store doors. Alfred's sleep deprivation was obvious on any day of week, and he was known to crack his head and glasses on the coffee table, or even fall off the stool behind the front counter during a lull in traffic. But I was wrong. Those of us who weren't there for the late night sessions didn't need to be. And those who were there, including Alfred, chose it above loneliness, taverns, alcohol, and maybe even the Democratic Party.

In its early years the store, with its hardware, machinery, post office, dry goods and groceries, was probably the Wal-Mart Supercenter of its time. But in the Golden Age of the Coffee Table, the mercantile wares had diminished, business and profits were down, and the store hours suggested things were out of control and getting worse.

But we fooled them. We fooled them all along. Even after many took most of their business to the big grocery stores in town, we fooled them (and maybe ourselves). It never was about selling groceries.

Chapter 3
"The McCaskey"

Aside from the coffee table, "The McCaskey" was the heart of the store, and unlike the coffee table it had something to do with the business of running the store. This unique piece of office furniture sat atop a long wooden counter, the end of which served as the check-out counter, the center being the McCaskey and a cash register. An assortment of candies sat on the section of counter that led to the front door of the store. Large drawers under the counter were mostly a stash for junk, old records, papers, and the occasional piece of merchandise that didn't merit display.

The McCaskey itself, from the store aisle, looked like a two foot square wooden billboard that served to shield customers from the heart of business operations. Community notices were taped in haphazard fashion for customers to see, including ads for well-drillers, loggers and other craftsmen; church dinners, and an assortment of cartoons, wise sayings, and political opinions that had been clipped from magazines or newspapers. Occasionally Aunt Ruth or Uncle Alfred would add to the collection with something that struck their particular religious or political inclination. Firm red underlining of the quote provided emphasis. Sometimes the quotes would have to be handwritten (since this was an era before copy machines), and the left-handed slant was a dead give-away of Uncle's work.

"The McCaskey"

The back of the McCaskey was a majestic center of business operations that rivaled the thrill and authority of an air traffic control room, at least in my mind when I was growing up in the store. Twelve metal sheets folded down in accordion fashion to reveal their front and back sides covered with ten spring loaded metal clips. The clips held the individual bills that customers had accumulated, since much of the store business operated on credit, with customers paying (hopefully) once every week or two. The first of the metal sheets didn't have clips on the outside; instead, it had various sized pieces of paper or cardboard taped for display so the register operator could read the most recent prices for oil, meats, vegetables and refrigerated items; basically the common goods that may not have been readily accessible. In front of the fold down sheets was a flat piece of framed glass (which miraculously was never broken in 90 years!). The glass allowed viewing of a tan faded sheet of paper that included the customer names in alpha order, noted with numbers to correspond to their numbered accounts within the accordion sheets. The paper record of customer names was taped to a pull out wooden slat so the aged record could be edited. I never recall the sheet being replaced, and as such it provided a history of the generations that frequented the store. In addition to being next to the cash register that needed some level of security, I instinctively knew this area of the store, that included the record of consumer debt, was confidential and I cringed whenever a customer would get a bit too friendly and step behind the counter for a closer view of this control center. But the design of the store had merchandise counters behind the register area also, so invasions to this area were common.

The base of the McCaskey was substantial since it had to support the heavy metal sheets, and held several drawers, none of which seemed to serve much purpose other than to randomly hold pens, pencils and other rarely used office paraphernalia. And, it served to be one more collection point for seldom, if ever, used goods that lacked categorization. In contrast to other storage nooks and crannies within the store, this collection point was undercover.

I imagine there were many versions of the stool that sat behind the McCaskey and the cash register. But the one I remember most was the tall, four legged, substantial swivel stool, with a red plastic seat cover (at least the parts that hadn't been cracked and covered with either black electrical tape or duct tape). I could sit atop the stool, swivel with contentment and survey the whole store, as well as look out the front window to see the gas pumps and the traffic cruising by on State Highway 82. Atop this stool one could appear in control and calmly wait for the customer to bring items to the counter for check out. And yes, there was a sense that one was actually providing a service to friends, neighbors and strangers, not unlike the coordination of an air traffic controller.

It was especially rewarding dealing with the closest local customers. Often they would pull out a new billing book from the drawer beneath the counter, write in their own items and politely ask us to check it. And the afterthought was, "Oh, say, I think my husband got a loaf of bread this morning and forgot to write it down. I better do that." It even went further than that. Some very close customers would come in the back door of the store on Sundays (the only time we weren't open), reach up above the door sill, deftly extract the hidden key that allowed entrance to the back room of the store, wander through the treacherous piles of tools and trash, and find their way to the front room of the store to grab some essentials. They would then write up the grocery items on their "bill" or a pad intentionally left on the check-out counter by Aunt Ruth, and be on their way. As one friend fondly recalled first engaging in this practice she said her surprise was not that she was able do so; after all, she was a close friend. Her surprise was when discovered she was not in the exclusive company she thought. She was the tenth person on the list that Sunday!

Learning about the store business involved careful observation, listening, and figuring out why things were done as they were. I observed that margarine was sold from a refrigerator in the back room (a personal refrigerator, not the one that customers had access to). Some people requested margarine for health reasons and we were happy to oblige, but to put it out in public was an affront to real butter and the local dairy business. The butter was rich and creamy, produced at a creamery within driving distance. One customer (who lived close by, and to our chagrin purchased very few other groceries) would stop by weekly for a pound of butter, pronouncing it "boooter," in a way that identified it as a special product and made you think a slab of the rich yellow cream was already on his tongue.

Nobody ever did a great job educating me about the facts of life in a deliberate manner, so with curiosity I observed that the sanitary napkins were much less visibly displayed than other products. They were shelved on the far wall, unobtrusively sandwiched between seldom called for products—a private collection of books that was sitting around gathering dust, and obscure handicrafts that never sold (but pleased the local artists because they were at least on display). The napkins, one brand only, were far enough away so the clerk could casually respond to the customer request, retrieve the product and unobtrusively slip it into a brown paper bag before it found its way back to the checkout counter. Having to follow through on this sales ritual was my greatest fear as I gradually moved toward clerking on my own. It never occurred to me to ask why we did it this way; I just grew into the knowledge that this was something very private. In retrospect, I suspect any answer to such a question would have left me relatively void of pertinent information anyway. (It would have been like the "birds and bees" book that I got from my aunt who ran the Bible Book Store in Viroqua, which, to no surprise, just told about the literal birds and bees and flowers, leaving the reader to make quantum leaps to any helpful and factual human information.) When the women would gather their own supplies, I was mostly able to avoid embarrassment, but when the bachelor farmer would come in and shop for personal products for his unmarried sister, and seek me out as the expert, it was an embarrassing stretch of my grade school clerking expertise. Fortunately I survived because I was accomplished with paper bags, and only had to choose from one product line.

Of course there had been a progression of jobs that led to the honor of sitting solo behind the McCaskey and "running the store." There had been the training of stocking the shelves, which mostly consisted of either pulling boxes of canned goods out from under the bottom shelves, or carrying the boxes in from the back room, provided they were not too heavy. Putting the cans onto the shelves was not a huge task, but the long narrow rows of Campbell's soup cans were often a challenge since the shelves could accommodate only a row, or two at the most, of the most popular (chicken noodle and tomato) varieties. Chicken gumbo or onion soup might only merit half a row, and consequently the remainder of their cases would be merged with another variety in a mixed 48-can carton below the shelf. Remembering what was in stock was fairly complex for a grade school kid, as well as anxiety producing when a customer called for the can of onion soup you knew was there, but could only be produced by pulling out five boxes in a search and find mission. Reaching to the back of a partial row, or slipping in between two deep rows would occasionally result in a crash and dents in the wooden shelving. The crash of tumbling cans was like a bomb had exploded, and the once quiet job gave way to exasperated looks of disapproval from the elders as if the fine china had been rolled down a set of stairs.

Perhaps the most unusual job was that of fly swatting. Frustrated by the onslaught of summer flies, Aunt Ruth negotiated the bounty of "a penny for each five flies." On a good day I could rack up enough in some of my killing rampages to buy a candy bar or two. There were rules of course. I couldn't hang out around the back screen door too much and let the prey in, and extra caution was dictated as I hunted the front of the store near the white painted metal bread rack. I couldn't hit the loaves of bread, and if I connected too directly with the flies, I had to wipe the blood up. It was a bit more sporty to hit them in mid air, but my sense of ethics, already well established, never allowed me to count a fly that had been catapulted over two aisles unless there was a body to prove a kill. Finding the kill was even more difficult when they landed, camouflaged, on the long black rubber mats that covered the main aisles of the wood floor. And I had to put all the flies in the trash, conveniently located next to the meat scale, which was a ripe killing field in itself. The best kills were slashing blows to flies on the edge of a counter – lethal strikes, with the victims falling bloodless to the floor below.

***

All was not rosy and simple when I had graduated to working the counter, particularly those times when I was alone in the store. Being alone was a feeling of authority, and onset of early adulthood and recognized competence – complete with the anxiety of responsibility, decisions, embarrassment, and problem solving. Strangers were the most anxiety producing, because invariably they wanted directions to some obscure site or farmhouse that was best described by phrases such as "just turn left at The Cottonwood Tree and go about a mile until you come to the Johnson farm…." They would leave with a "thanks, I think I can find it now." A slight feeling of incompetence and failed

responsibility emerged as they headed off in exactly the op-
posite direction of The Cottonwood Tree. But that tree
was a well established local landmark for many generations,
and a directional tool used by all the local adults, so why
shouldn't the store trainee be able to give the same descriptive account to get strangers further lost?

Strangers also had the bad habit of asking for something you didn't have in stock, or they wanted another brand
name than rested on the shelves. Two brands of baked
beans or tuna simply was not a luxury afforded in a country
store. If you wanted variety, you could always take a loaf of
the cracked-wheat, rather than the fluffy white Sunbeam
bread. Worse than not having the product was the need
to search for the item in "the back room." Granted, it was
only a few feet behind the cash register, accessed via a time
worn light green wooden door (that always held the largest
of calendars), but I could never feel perfectly comfortable
leaving the customers alone—particularly the shady looking teen-agers—near the candy, cigarettes or cash register. Instinctively one knew that folks fell into three catego-
ries: perfectly trustworthy friends, those you would take
a chance on, and those you would never leave alone. The
latter category included a subset that could be described as
"the greasy-haired (in search of cigarettes) late adolescent
male who appeared to be out of high school but for reasons
other than graduation." It was easy enough to deny that
you carried something if you didn't want to go to the back
room, but not so easy to deny the request that you go outside the front door and pump five gallons of gasoline. The
strategy was to pump the gas fast, standing erect, facing the

large glass store front, and make your presence at pump appear like it extended to the swivel stool behind the counter. I think it usually worked, but our inventory system would have never confirmed it unless you absolutely knew there was only one pack of Marlboros left in the tobacco rack.

Strangers were also the ones who didn't know that "it just doesn't work that way." It was strangers who would think that a fill of gasoline merited a windshield wash like the real gas stations in town. When that happened, depending on our mood, we might scurry to the back room and scrounge up rag and a bottle of Windex to appease them. Some were grateful and recognized at that point that you had gone the extra mile – and they quickly became long term friends; others never thought twice, labeled us as "country hicks," and remained strangers.

Since the store was a public place, it wasn't unusual that the act of meeting strangers was more like a courting ritual than a formal "hand-shaking I want to meet you" kind of place. A handshake was rare, something left for preachers, but lots of head nodding to acknowledge whatever informal introduction had taken place. Names would eventually surface, maybe when you gently asked a visitor several minutes into the conversation. The conversations would begin safely, like, "I think my father maybe used to stop here when he used to pass through on his way to the river. Would that have been your parents that ran the store back then?" Or, "So, it looks like quite of bit of tobacco across the road. I knew they had a tobacco co-op up in Viroqua, but wasn't just sure where the stuff was raised." Eventually the conversation would flow to the inevitable response, "and would you maybe like a cup of coffee?"

Strangers were also sometimes uncomfortable when hospitality was offered. Tired, or lost, when offered a cup of coffee, there was often a hesitancy to accept. Was it an attempt to sell coffee or lure an unsuspecting soul into an uncomfortable religious conversation? Sometimes they would leave some change on the coffee table in the back of the store, and wander out wondering what the motives were, and remain strangers. Others would linger a bit longer and discover something unique about the store, its owners, or "the regulars" at the coffee table. Those strangers, although they didn't fit into the local radius of customers, would manufacture reasons to stop at the store in the future: gas, some special Farley's hot dogs that you couldn't buy in town, or a loaf of bread while passing through. But they knew they were no longer strangers and gently sent signals (like a longing look at the coffee table and its fresh cookies) that they would be grateful to sit down and share in the communal table. Years later when the store finally closed its doors, even this group found its way back to say thank-you to a home away from home that had welcomed them many years ago. Or sometimes it was the wife, whose husband was now gone, but wanted us to know that he always talked about this oasis of coffee and relaxed, undemanding hospitality.

***

While many of the stories of what happened behind the McCaskey are lost, it continues to tell the story of the store. For lack of a proper home for display, it sits in my basement closet. It was one of the few items that held an emotional attachment for me prior to the finality of an auction block that scattered much of the store history. Within the black enveloping metal sheets still remain yellowed account slips that reflect unpaid bills dating back to the years of World War I, chronicling the prices of gas, shoes, bread, and the occasional trade value for a load of wood or carton of eggs.

I have only a vague recollection of the word "dun" from my youth. I only heard it on rare occasion, and assumed it was something like its homonym, "done," and referred to Aunt Ruth being tired and "done" with the seemingly fruitless efforts when she engaged in a sporadic tirade to clean out the overdue accounts and hold debtors accountable. One faded envelope behind the number "40" clip in the McCaskey was labeled "duns," with several names on it. A check with the dictionary clarifies that the word referred to her repeated attempts to demand payment for accounts.

Inside the envelope was a brief glimpse of Mr. B, whose $25.55 bill from 1963 included numerous 30 cent packs of cigarettes, bread at the same price, 39 cent Malt-O-Meal, and gas at a price that informed the infamous country song: *Back When Gas Was 30 Cents a Gallon, Love Was Only 60 Cents Away.* Mr. B's name conjures up terms such as deadbeat, probably a term no longer politically correct, but one that back then was unsympathetically associated with those who couldn't bring themselves to stability or accountability – and it was often associated with alcohol. The reinforcing clue to this value judgment of Mr. B, probably left by Uncle Alfred, was a tiny newspaper clipping dated three years later in 1996 that listed Mr. B's street address in Lacrosse, and noted an $18 fine for failing to dim his headlights. It remains a possibility that the article was clipped for a last known address; but it was more likely a note for the file that confirmed we got stiffed on a debt by someone who could afford a traffic fine, but ignore an honest retailer.

A more poignant story was also in that envelope. Mrs. C and her family apparently moved from the area in late 1957. The carbon copy from our Underwood typewriter records the first letter from the Allen Halverson Store dated January 27, 1958:

> Enclosed is the amount you are owing the store. The check you wrote out on Saturday, the 18th, is included. I sent it to bank the first of the following week, but they said the account was closed and returned the check.

> The reason I didn't keep asking you to pay your bill was because I thought you would take care of it before you went. You were honest about it before and I trusted you and also told others I believed you would do the right thing.

> It's tax time and also we have to pay cash for all our groceries so we need the money. Thank you.

The bad check is also in the file, signed and dated by Mrs. C. It was the generic blank check variety that store-keepers kept in their drawers; customers would simply ask if you had a check blank from local establishments such as the DeSoto State Bank. All a patron had to do was fill in the date, amount, and sign it – the familiar signature was good enough to draw on an account. Mrs. C. responded on February 25, 1958:

> *Dear Ruth, We will pay our bill as soon as we get over that way. Hope you don't think we don't want to pay it. Mrs. C*

The following letter dated more than three years later of August 18, 1961 elicited a $5 payment on September 12:

> *In regard to your bill at the store here at West Prairie— we have a copy of the letter written to you on January 27, 1958 and the answer you sent on February 25, 1958 saying you would pay.*
>
> *As of yet we have received no payment on your account which includes the check you wrote without an account in the DeSoto State Bank and now it is August 1961.*
>
> *We need the money – if you decide to pay so much a month that is ok, but please decide one way or another. We don't like to force payments, but that is what we are doing in some cases.*
>
> *Thank you. Allen Halverson Store*

The last letter from Mrs. C was dated February 9, 1962:

Dear Sir,
It has been swell of you to be so patient for our money. It
has been hard to pay our bill as he has been either been
laid up with a broken leg or laid off from his job. He has
been out of work off & on about 3 years out of four &
with 10 children it hasn't been easy. He should be going
back to work the 1st part of April & I'll send the rest of
the bill then. Thanks again, Mrs. C

No other record is noted. Maybe it was that letter
that moved the account of $28.94 into the "duns" envelope,
but I am inclined to think Aunt Ruth had moved it sympa-
thetically to her really "done" file.

There are many remaining account slips in the McCaskey, most of them simply reflecting long overdue accounts
and entertaining historical records of prices. But one account stands out, thicker than any of the others, and the accounting such that the final tally was really in doubt. It was
dated 1968, the year I moved off to college. The account
was in my father's name. Maybe the date was coincidence
and that date just happened to be when they stopped the
artificial tallying of my family's financial debts to the store—
in final recognition that this was a communal existence that
blurred business, family, and community ventures. The financial accounting really doesn't matter – but the debt I
owe to the store is still unpaid and my old friend, the Mc-
Caskey, provides that reminder.

Chapter 4
Out of Place

They just didn't fit. The family came into the store one day and expressed an interest in '"trading" at the store; not literally as trading had occurred in previous generations (eggs for flour, etc.), but trading simply to mean a place for them to purchase groceries. Even using that term, however, suggested something of a throwback or backwoods nature. They weren't part of the immediate farm community and had no friends in West Prairie, making their presence highly unusual.

Their appearance was also unusual. They were a ragtag family of obviously limited educational, intellectual and financial means, with relationships that were hard to define. The unkempt matriarch was a middle aged, overweight woman whose appearance suggested that she had never purchased new clothing, or experienced the luxuries of a stylist for her greasy black hair. She would have benefited from the services of a dentist, but that luxury was likely more difficult to access than their absent medical care. She led the rest of the family, including three children. A curious adolescent boy, dressed in dirty clothes, politely explored the store and his obese older sister assisted her mother with the shopping. The youngest, a quiet blonde toddler, had an innocent beauty that begged the unnerving question of what the future would hold for her. The two older men that accompanied the group (and that seemed to be their primary role), had little to say, and would have been easy marks for a caricature artist portraying lean and scruffy displaced guys in overalls, vacant faced, with toothless grins. We were surprised when we discovered which one was the matriarch's father and which one was her husband.

Uncle Alfred and Aunt Ruth took them on as customers, despite assuming that they were in West Prairie because they had worn out their credit welcome elsewhere. We never really knew. They always showed up as a family and were never part of the coffee crowd that sat at the coffee table, mostly because they had little in common with anyone else who shared in the store community. But they came to the store in their overcrowded and overworked car on a regular basis. The large quantities they purchased would have been much more consistent with a grocery trip to a city store, rather than to the limited offerings available in West Prairie. That would have required cash. We offered credit, not unlimited, but credit nonetheless, to a family that had need. Twenty or forty dollars might be applied weekly, with the total bill creeping higher.

They were slightly strange but friendly. Conversations were mostly one way, from them to us as if we might be the only people that listened to the happenings of their provincial daily life. Some talk about their ramshackle house. Some talk about their gardens. An upcoming wedding. It was hard to imagine who their friends might have been.

At Christmas, Uncle Alfred was the recipient of a 59 cent bottle of Mennen's Aftershave, purchased from our own shelf.

I find myself reflecting on how we treated them, and to what extent we respected them. We listened some, extended credit, and at least superficially treated them with dignity. But their oddities and poverty prompted some "us and them" thinking in my mind. Maybe we had met "the other" where they were at. It's hard to say.

And then one day, with no explanation, they just stopped coming to the store, possibly ashamed of being unable to pay their escalating debt, or thinking they had finally reached the end of their credit line. We never knew what happened to them.

I think about the bottle of aftershave more than I think of the debt.

Chapter 5
Danger and Despair

It all started innocently enough. Aunt Aleda decided to discard her dilapidated, mixed and incomplete set of golf clubs that cluttered her Chicago efficiency apartment. Any home that centrally featured a Murphybed certainly didn't have the spatial luxury to have a set of unused clubs sitting around in storage. Where she got them is a mystery, probably a remnant of her more leisurely days as a Navy nurse during the off days of World War II. Whatever, she discarded them to her nephews in West Prairie. Some were irons that were all iron, but there were some that had a wooden shaft (quickly susceptible to breakage which happened soon into the acquisition), and a few mismatched woods that seemed to be there just to call it a set.

Life in the country frequently called for improvisation, so it wasn't a far stretch, given that the country farms had no greens or fairways without cow pies in the summertime, that winter golf would crop into our minds. One could have a pretty entertaining afternoon with the firmly crusted snow (so firm you could walk on it) and some red lipstick on the balls. Although "greens" were hard to define, there was no problem poking a few holes in the snow, providing you didn't poke so deep that a sunken ball would sink far into the softer white powder a few inches beneath the surface. That scenario would lead to a cold hand, or even a lost ball that we had delusions of finding when spring arrived. Attempting to drive the ball was a bit harder than putting, but if one connected, it was a sure recipe for lost balls as they skimmed for miles across the white terrain.

So when summer arrived, neighbor Al and I thought that experimenting in some place other than pasture would preserve the balls and finely hone our limited skills. The store itself was positioned so there was only about ten yards between the store and County Road N on the west, and State Highway 82 to the north. But to the east, was a large well mown yard that many years ago had housed sheds for the machinery and automobile dealerships that once were part of store operations. We positioned ourselves at the end of the yard, close to the township storage sheds and sand piles, about 90 yards from the large east face of the store. We posited that a well hit ball, which was well beyond our wildest dreams, would simply hit the side of the store.

And the first ten swings resulted in dribbled and dubbed balls that were easily found within the first twenty yards of lawn. But finally success screamed off the driver (actually, the first of a lifetime of slices) and my ball sailed toward the north end of the store, headed somewhat toward the two gas pumps and a car that sat in front of the store. Unfortunate timing had Sylvia, the neighbor lady who lived across the highway, exiting the front of the store about the time the ball left the tee. How the projectile managed to fly between the pumps, car and Sylvia without as much as a bounce or whistle being noticed was a wonder never discussed with anyone. We half-heartedly searched for the lost golf ball in the ditches kitty-corner from the store to no avail, mostly thinking of the disasters nearly avoided. And our taste for the city person's game never really surfaced in the country again.

Al was indirectly responsible for another near disaster and two serious life lessons, since he was the neighbor that Uncle Alfred sought to keep up with, on my behalf. Lesson number one was, "Don't try to keep up with the Joneses." Al generally had access to all the new toys and gadgets well before anyone else in the neighborhood, so when he became the owner of a highly envied go-cart, Alfred devised one of the more ill-fated, albeit creative, mechanical schemes that ever graced the prairie. The concept was simple; deconstruct several good working pieces of machinery in order to cobble together a mode of transport that could never be recreated, and clearly upstage the lowly go-cart ground level transportation.

The first machine to undergo transition was my 24 inch, purple and white Schwinn bicycle. Its stable frame basically remained intact except for the holes cut through the rear luggage carrier. And atop the carrier was a jerry rigged metal slat platform that served as the mount for the soul of the other machine that lost its entire identity – a Toro lawnmower. The Briggs and Stratton engine, once having been removed from the mower, was carefully welded and mounted with nuts and bolts to the luggage carrier. The drive shaft, now separated from the mower blades, was fitted with a small wheel and positioned slightly offset to the right side, to align as the top end of a pulley system with another small wheel that had been affixed to the rear wheel axle of my Schwinn. A throttle-type cable device was mounted on the bar between the bike seat and handle-bars. It didn't really serve as a throttle but functioned to engage or disengage the belt tension between the motor and wheel.

Instead of a few pulls with a rope, the Briggs and Stratton engine could now be started when the driver peddled the Schwinn to sufficient speed and deftly engaged the throttle, which resulted in the pulley system turning over the engine. Aside from the awkwardness and balance problems of peddling hard and using only one hand to stabilize the bike while also pushing the throttle cables with the other hand, the starting system was a mechanical success. The bike was christened the "Izzer," a take-off on the commercial Whizzer motorbike.

Both my brother Dave and I were able to negotiate trial runs of the newly engineered motorbike down the smooth and flat surfaces of County Highway N. It was on a sunny Sunday morning after church services that we decided a bit more adventurous trip was in order, so the direction was west on State Highway 82. Minimum destination was to go past the Rust farm, about ½ mile from the store, where I could undoubtedly impress those neighbors who happened to have a daughter of my age. Dave, riding his regular bicycle, quickly fell behind the new wonder, and was still headed west in my direction after I had successfully turned the bike around and headed for home. Unfortunately as I returned, the road presented a slight downhill slope, and as I naturally began to accelerate speed, the flaws of design became apparent. An elevated heavy weight, positioned slightly off center on a light, fast moving object is destined for unpredictable happenings. The last thing I remembered before I found myself underneath the bike and motor—with the motor burning a hole in my back—was my luggage carrier motor swaying back and forth as if it was hoping to jump off into one of the roadside ditches. Lesson number one about keeping up with the Joneses, now had a corollary, "…it could be dangerous." Lesson number two was simple, "Don't mess with the laws of aerodynamics; it is dangerous."

Dave pulled me from beneath the bike and managed to carry me on his bike back to our penthouse home, and soon my parents were driving me to the emergency room in Viroqua. My religious sentiments on the journey were pretty much along the lines of being thankful that the disaster was not any worse, and maybe an internal recognition that grace sometimes includes painful warning as the outcome for ill-conceived ideas. My mother reports that our family doctor, simply known as Dr. Lars, didn't need to communicate much more that an incredulous shake of his head as the story was recounted to him. I spent the better part of Sunday afternoon in the emergency room getting stitches sown in my head, burns tended to, and bits of gravel extracted from various body sites.

That evening I rested in my bed with a throbbing headache, and in the background heard the lyrical march from the television as Alfred Hitchcock walked into his facial outline. On that Sunday night, the *Funeral March of a Marionette* could have been easily replaced by a funeral dirge for a naïve grade school kid. And about that time, my Uncle Alfred was returning from one of his Sunday ventures to Iowa. His own march was trudging and methodical as he climbed up the long stairway to our apartment, to greet family and deliver a copy of the Sunday Des Moines Register. He fell silent as the account of the day's misadventures was told. After stopping in my room, with few words spoken, he left. Apologies weren't common in my family; penitence was like a dog with its tail between its legs, more likely expressed by silence and retreat.

***

The storefront gas pumps were not always as lucky as they, and Sylvia had been on that day when they escaped a screaming golf ball. One would think that the traffic dangers of being at the crossing of two roads made the store vulnerable, or at least put at risk those who had to enter or cross the state highway from the lesser county road. But I recall no major vehicle collisions because of the intersection itself. People were careful since, particularly from the south, the visibility was limited by the crest of a hill. The dangers seemed to be presented by strangers who screamed through the countryside, ignoring the posted and reduced speed limit of the unincorporated village.

One afternoon the store was shaken by a resounding crash, only a second after one of the gas pumps was seen flying into mid air. The scraping and grinding of an automobile hitting the gas pump and concrete base protectors was lost in the rumbling jolt that ripped the northeast corner of the store. Double fortune had no cars in front of the store, and my mother happening to be in the store at the time. She calmly grabbed the large silver and copper trimmed fire extinguisher that was stationed behind the front counter and next to the back room door, and rushed to the storefront where a fire had begun to emerge from the hole where the gas pump formerly stood. I viewed my mother slightly differently after that encounter. Never before had I thought of her using bad judgment or being brave; I still don't know which of those traits defined her actions that afternoon, but the fire was miraculously extinguished, the corner of the store mended, and the gas pump eventually replaced. The crash also prompted the transfer of the kerosene pump that had been located inside the store, at the northeast corner crash site, to an outside location. One of my childhood jobs now became more I difficult. I needed to go outside in the cold winter months to pump the kerosene that fueled the heating stove in our upstairs apartment. Life went on.

On another occasion my father was the rescuer when a car, the driver probably asleep or having accidentally braked out of control when the intersection was noted as a potential danger, flashed by the storefront, skidded through driveway and yard, rolled, and eventually rested in the pond 150 yards from the store. What exactly happened in the rescue is unclear, but my memory is that of my father riding in the sheriff's station wagon ambulance, holding onto the man until he was deposited in the safe confines of the emergency room. This accident was the most visible manifestation of the store being a respite in time of crisis for strangers. But for years the store, and especially my father, catered to those with broken down vehicles and flat tires (in an era when they weren't a rare occurrence). It was never defined as an intrusion or opportunity, just something accepted in the role of hospitality to the stranger at the crossroads.

While full blown tragedy had been avoided with car crashes at the crossroads, tragedies were not strangers to the farming community. Farm accidents claimed limbs; tractors rolled and killed the operators; neighbors were lost in logging accidents. A church and community leader died in a hay baling accident. And there was the suicide of a depressed farmer across the ridge. The store was the center for the community to communicate and share the bad news. "Why the big crowd at so and so's farm? Did you hear about the accident? Can you tell me what happened? What can we do to help? Who is going to take care of the cows?"

And Sylvia, who years before had escaped the golf ball near the storefront gas pumps, eventually lost her aging husband at the very same spot. It was night and he was crossing the road to have dinner in the store, probably preoccupied with the thoughts of some warm oyster stew and the usual camaraderie. Everyone conjectured that his hearing was such that he never heard the car coming over the crest of the hill. Nobody ever blamed the driver. There was an irony in the sudden death when he was simply seeking a safe haven and friendship. Somehow living at the crossroads seemed to suggest a metaphor of how life was meant to be lived, with the opportunity for relationships, new ventures, new people, and a possible window to someplace else. But it never exempted those who entered the crossroads from the risks and the inescapable realities of a full life that included disappointment, tragedy and death.

Beyond just living with death, tragedy and personal losses, the store was a repository for grief. It gathered and lived there because this was the heart of the community. Grief hung in the air sometimes, like it does at a church or funeral; but it remained, and eventually found itself being absorbed into the dark stained coffee table, like the coffee that had been spilled. The long blank stares that sometimes accompanied a cup of coffee were often accepted with the silent outpouring of another half cup.

Chapter 6
Christmas

Frost draped the huge window pane that was bordered with colorful stained glass squares. In contrast to other times of the year when the window accentuated the deteriorating physical frame of the store, with chipped paint and rusted metal window braces, the northwest corner of the store with its wintry glass served to festively host a small twinkling Christmas tree, playful Christmas villages and a nativity scene, all gently resting in the angel fluff snow that filled the wide window seat. Christmas had replaced boxes of jersey gloves, rubber footwear, and the ashtrays that supported the Saturday night fellowship.

Christmas was a special time in the store. Holiday baking brought the local farmwives in for flour and other essentials, and the fruits of their labor fed the abundant array of Christmas goodies at the coffee table. For some the treats were just an extension of their normally generous food offerings to the coffee crowd. For others, the food was a year end appreciation for a whole year of hospitality. Sometimes something elaborate beyond the plate of decorated Christmas cookies would arrive, such as fancy meat and cheese trays, special boxed candies and nuts. Fruit cakes that were received were nibbled at by Aunt Ruth and a few women patrons of the coffee table (but merited comedic rejection from the men). And the occasional card with a twenty dollar bill was an obvious recognition of 52 weeks of coffee drinking.

It was also the time of year to express appreciation to friends and customers for their patronage, usually by means of a simple calendar that bore a non-descript picture with the store name stamped on the bottom so it could be seen for the whole year. Alfred and Ruth annually scratched out a list of the regular customers that seemed deserving, and ordered a few extra in case they had forgotten someone or wanted to share with friends outside the community. Alfred was the primary dispenser of the calendars and with a gentle smile would reach into the drawer beneath the check-out counter to present the gifts. These would never become valued collectables, in contrast to the premiums of a more prosperous era. The smaller two inch calendars, accompanied by a classic picture with perhaps a thermometer attached to the side were popular for many years. The ones surviving to this day suggest that they were appreciated for aesthetic reasons and rarely defaced by crassly ripping off the miniscule monthly sheets. On the more extravagant end, suggesting even more prosperous years, was a Red Wing Pottery mixing bowl, with *COME TO WEST PRAIRE, TRADE WITH ALLEN HALVERSON*, stamped in deep blue letters on the inside bottom of the bowl.

Despite being the heart of the community, there was little activity in gift sales, mostly because there weren't many products that lent themselves to gift giving. On occasion there would be a pair of leather gloves sold, or even an inexpensive bottle of after-shave lotion for the last minute and less than affluent shopper. But without a doubt the biggest retail item of the season was lutefisk, the sun-dried, and then lye soaked codfish, that was an entrenched part of the local Norwegian heritage. At some point in time, the actual lye solution had given way to other soaking agents, but it made no difference. Nothing could compare to this strange fish; the biblical pun was that it was "the piece of cod that passes understanding."

Uncle Alfred would annually order multiple 50 pound round metal/cardboard tubs of the soaking fish and methodically sort out the fish by size and perceived quality, package them in smaller plastic bags, and sell (or give) them to the customers who depended on this annual tradition. Alfred and some self proclaimed local experts would always evaluate the quality of the fish, visually, and of course, by the smell. The underground joke, usually told apart from the women, was that the quality of the fish (post consumption) was confirmed by the extent to which the "farts burned your eyes." The Norwegian response to such a joke would be a chuckle and the traditional Norse "uff da!"

The fish was prepared by wrapping the fish pieces in cheesecloth and gently boiling it until just the correct amount of gelling occurred. Not enough boiling would leave a chewy and strong tasting fish. Too much would result in a mushy substance that reminded the consumer of glue. Correct boiling would fill the air with a sharp and distinctive odor, and provide a flaky, jelly textured fish that could be placed on a flat roll of lefse, covered with butter and salt, and enjoyed with communal conversation. The conversation was not as refined as a wine tasting, but critique of the quality and texture always happened, and was followed by the compliments of the lefse.

The lefse (comparable to an extremely large and thin soft tortilla), also a Norwegian tradition, was almost always from a local kitchen, and never criticized, but careful note was taken in regard to the thickness and whether it was potato lefse or otherwise. Lefse baking was considered an art form, and unlike other baking ventures, was practiced by only a few women of Norwegian heritage who had the proper kitchen supplies and skills. Commercial lefse, however, was fair game for criticism, and however good, was never elevated to the status of the local cooks.

But getting to the point of eating the traditional meal of lutefisk on Christmas Eve was a test of patience. My family practiced gift opening on Christmas Eve, but not until after the meal and the dishes had been washed. The prelude to the dinner preparation was the closest thing to torture of my early childhood experience (with the possible exception of trips to the dentist). Christmas Eve was always busy in the store with some last minute grocery shopping (particularly for lutefisk), so I would wait in anticipation, upstairs in our penthouse apartment, peering out the front window. I wished away the cars parked in front of the store, and watched the snow fly by the gas pumps, only to see one more car arrive and know that our country store wasn't anything like the conversation void convenience stores of the modern era. Store "hours" didn't really exist, or more accurately, were never adhered to, so closing the doors, even on Christmas Eve, was still a hit and miss proposition. And when Alfred did get to the point of closing, it was then, and only then, that he would find some of the best hunks of lutefisk for our celebration. With some luck, the timing coincided with my father's completion of milking and evening farm chores.

At other times of the year the ever present open door practice of the store was mostly an inconvenience. But on Christmas Eve, the store could feel like an intrusion to *most* of the family.

So I waited, and waited. Aunt Aleda always came home for Christmas from her nursing profession in Chicago, and it was undoubtedly her brainchild that it wouldn't be breaking the rules if the kids could open one present before dinner. This made the wait somewhat bearable, but selecting that one present was also a challenge. I wanted to pick a good present, one that would excite me and keep the anticipation alive, but not one that I might perceive as the Number One present, that would minimize the gifts to come. A present from Aunt Aleda was the safest bet (and she was willing to help in the selection) because she always gave multiple gifts – and good ones. There was no losing in picking one that either was in the entertainment (games/toys) category, or new clothes. Clothing may not have seemed to be exciting to many kids my age, but her taste was always good and nurtured by the experts in Marshall Fields of downtown Chicago. So my brother and I, despite being low income, were fashionably dressed and even elicited comment from the impressed school secretaries, thanks to gifts from

Aunt Aleda and additional aunts and uncles that resided in Chicago and on the east coast, and frequented the likes of Bloomingdales and Carson Pierre Scott.

Dinner finally came to our penthouse with multiple helpings of lutefisk and lefse, some frozen corn, pickles; and an abundance of meatballs, gravy and mashed potatoes for those of us who couldn't conceive of making a whole meal of the gelatin-like fish. Perhaps meatballs and mashed potatoes with multiple helpings of lefse, intricately rolled with lots of real butter and possibly some jelly, would have satisfied me, but as a child of Scandinavian heritage I felt an obligation to have a small serving of fish rolled up in the lefse with a generous portion of salt and butter.

Christmas Eve dinner was one of the only meals of the year where it seemed the sex role stereotyping of women doing the kitchen clean-up was bypassed. By the time dinner was done, the anticipation of presents and my persistence to move things forward drove others into action. At the designated time, I would sort out the presents in piles and wait for the gift opening ritual. It followed a predictable rhythm, each of us taking a turn to open, with extra turns for my brother and me since we got the most presents. Each would take their time honored positions around the room. My brother and I would be nearest the front window near the Christmas tree; and even at that late hour I would glance over the branches, on the lookout for another car that might pull up in front of the store. Aunt Ruth and Aunt Aleda would settle into the timeworn couch. Mother was seated in a small chair across the room. Next to her in a soft sofa chair sat my father, closest to the less than realistic electric fireplace, who would find a small notepad and pencil to methodically record all his gifts. Uncle Alfred, seated somewhat away from the group on a wooden chair in the adjacent dining room, would pull out his jackknife and painstakingly slice through the cellophane tape of each package and dutifully fold the wrapping paper for future use, but not without a careful critique of the paper that nearly rivaled his lutefisk analysis. Years later I finally noted the irony of his paper conservation, because if he ever got beyond giving cards with twenty dollar bills inserted, his presents would be unceremoniously presented (late, after he would trek back down the stairs into the store to find a forgotten item) in large brown paper bags. The last of the presents gave way to the Christmas wrapping being gathered and disposed of (with special attention by my father to ensure nothing of value, especially envelopes with money, found its way into the trash bags), the floor was cleared, and the circus ring atmosphere emerged as we began the annual testing of electronic devices such as battery powered mechanical dogs who had made their way from the "Chicago Loop" department stores to the humble West Prairie Store.

The store had been closed since 7:30 pm. Uncle Alfred had been the last to leave and join the family in its Christmas festivities. The store would find respite from visitors for the next 35 hours – nobody knocking on the door, nobody tending the counter, no coffee. Nobody even sneaking in the back door.

Alfred announced his return to an empty store after all the packages had been opened, each thank-you expressed, and paper wrappings folded and discarded. Maybe he should check to see if the coffee pot was unplugged, get a few items he needed for Christmas Day. Good night.

I don't know what really happened in the store for the next two hours. Maybe he drank a lukewarm cup of coffee from the pot that he actually, to his surprise, had unplugged. Then an unplanned brief nap that was interrupted by a quick snap of the neck. And, oh yes, a search for several special Christmas cards that he had tucked away months before. A final check of the lutefisk bins to see if anything would be left for New Year festivities. I would like to think that one of those Christmas miracles took place, where inanimate objects briefly come to life. In this case the coffee table surveys the dark aisles of the store to be sure they are alone, and whispers "Merry Christmas my friend" in a gentle blessing that eases his lonely trek through the fresh fallen snow, across the road, to an empty farmhouse.

***

Miracle on 34th Street, It's a Wonderful Life, and *A Christmas Carol* are classic Christmas movies, with good reason. The associations and memories of these movies evoke multiple Christmas and personal emotions. But none conjure up the memories of Christmas for me as much as the unlikely choice of *The Wizard of Oz.* It remains somewhat of a puzzle why this classic movie was shown on what appeared to be a designated Sunday every year preceding the Christ-

mas season. But it was invariably shown on a Sunday afternoon, and seen in dramatic black and white (on, naturally
a black and white television set), in the backroom of the
store. Dorothy, the Wicked Witch of the West, and the
rest of the cast were in the backroom entertaining Uncle
Alfred, my brother Dave, and me as we enacted the most
secret Christmas ritual of West Prairie.

It was a generally unknown and unappreciated ritual
– and that is exactly what made it memorable and mysteriously meaningful. Certainly most of the North West Prairie
Lutheran Church, one half mile down the road, knew that
the apple and peanut treats for the annual Christmas program came from the store, but nobody knew or could have
bothered to seriously ponder how they were packaged on
the afternoon prior to the evening program.

There was a certain mystery to this production, since
Uncle Alfred was essentially, and seemingly bitterly, divorced
from the local church (though he found churches across the
state border in Iowa to meet some of his needs). But it was
never questioned that this job would be done; perhaps it
was just business. One of his other unknown acts related to
the church was making an annual payment of one dollar to
the church that he no longer attended. Sources suggested
that he did this to technically remain a legally contributing
member so he could be buried in the church cemetery.

The backroom of the store was mostly unheated and
thus the logical site for stacking the purple, red and white
cartons of Washington Delicious apples. Unlike the unpre-

dictable apples of the grocery stores today, these were always crisp and true to their name.

The best perk of the job was to sample the wares. Large burlap bags of peanuts and small brown paper bags were positioned to complete the small assembly line. There was a bit of risk in sampling the peanuts, since the ill placed shells could attract mice and invoke the ire of Aunt Ruth when she came to the store Monday morning. So we mostly stayed with apple sampling.

The first step was to put a scoop of peanuts in a paper bag. My recollection is that whatever we used for a scoop vaguely resembled the metal scoop that we used for the red sweeping compound that was periodically (and conservatively) sprinkled before sweeping the floors and rubber mats of the store. Exactness and fairness were the rules for the peanut level in the bag. Fairness in volume was the right way to distribute Christmas treats at a church Christmas program, and exactness was needed to ensure room for the apple that was delicately placed on top on the peanuts before the bag was carefully folded and stapled shut. Dave and I got peanut, bag, and staple duty.

The apples were reserved for Uncle Alfred. Of course he called the shots as the chief proprietor of the store, and organized the assembly line and duly assumed the patriarchal role of apple inspector. Not one apple with blemish (granted, there were very few of that sort) escaped his watchful eye as he gently unpacked each corrugated cardboard layer of apples from the carton, unwrapped each apple from its tissue paper, and then performed the meticulous (and hidden in the back room) act of individual apple polishing. This went on for hours, or so it seemed, and by job completion the allure of television viewing and apple sampling had worn thin.

Backs were tired and the stapled bags were carefully tucked back into the boxes and box covers, just about the time that the Wicked Witch was melting and Dorothy was on her way back to Kansas. The identity of The Wizard was revealed, and despite Dorothy's initial tirade to the contrary that he was a "very, very bad man," he revealed himself not as a bad man, just a bad wizard.

The church Christmas program had evolved over the years. No longer were the adult males stationed beside the Christmas tree with long poles and wet rags ready to douse any accidental fires caused by the real live candle decorations. Artificial Christmas lights and tinsel now adorned the tree, and the children's program and pageantry had become less concerned with solemnity (although still sacred). But the program always ended with the communal singing of *Silent Night*, followed by gift distribution. The Christmas tree, reaching all the way to the high church ceiling, like those in homes, was a gathering point for gifts. Families made sure that each child in the congregation had something under the tree, and the drama unfolded as a designated reader called out the names of present recipients. It was also the best way to send Christmas cards and friendly Christmas packages to neighbors. Of course, it was never guaranteed that everyone would get a present, especially the adults.

But that is where the bag of apple and peanuts came in. Everyone got something at Christmas.

Years later when Uncle Alfred died, he *was* buried in the church cemetery. For some, there were remaining mysteries that surrounded his life. But the sometimes hidden identity of Uncle Alfred, along with the Wizard, had been revealed many years earlier to his nephews in the back room of the store when he performed the sacred ritual of apple polishing.

Chapter 7
Candy

The store had two candy counters, one as customers came into the store and progressed down the aisle toward the cash register and check out counter, and the second behind the check out counter. The first held all the penny candies, cellophane sacks of Brach candies, and bagged nuts. Peanuts had a few regular customers, and even one high school student who would empty the small plastic sack of shelled and salted nuts in his Coca-Cola bottle for a crunchy pick-me-upper that served to grind the dark sugar water into his teeth. The bagged candies were on a small metal rack, turnover was limited, and mostly served to occupy space, except for special times of the year when someone might think the variety of bagged candies fit well into a holiday theme.

But the essential objective of the candy counter was to provide a variety of penny offerings that enthralled the younger visitors. Bubble gum, gumballs, malted milk balls and wide range of miscellaneous and frequently changing items were at eyelevel for the young customers, not unlike the current check-out counters of Wal-Mart and every grocery store in the country. Today those candy racks are simply money making distractions that drive parents near the brink of insanity, but in West Prairie they provided a true shopping experience for the young, wide eyed candy connoisseurs who made critical decisions with the two or three pennies they had been given. The staple of the aisle was cellophane wrapped penny "suckers"—simply a sugary hard-candy in oval shape, but with a rope-like loop handle, that after a few licks became soft and resulted in a sugar coated glob on tiny fingers – but at least falling and ramming a hard stick into the back of a throat was avoided.

And the candy cigarettes accompanied the penny candies. Chesterfield and Lucky Strikes were packed in a paper boxes whose label and packaging closely mimicked the real thing, except lacking the cellophane wrapping, and having only ten cigarettes compared to twenty of the authentic brown weed product. The white candy sticks, complete with red tips to simulate fire, were softer than hard candy canes, and could easily be popped into the mouth sideways, with the effect of bulging out both cheeks. But a few rolls of the tongue would soften and weaken the center of the stick, it would break, and led to about three or four good crunches before the next cigarette was extracted from the box. Since this was the preferred method of consumption, it might have been interesting research to establish if this particular confection led users to pop real cigarettes fully into their mouths, thereby creating tobacco chewers instead of smokers. Or perhaps an aspiring smoker might have inserted a lighted cigarette sideways into his mouth, thereby promoting lifelong avoidance.

Political correctness hadn't reached rural America during the 50's, but there was enough intuitive thinking to question if it was a good idea to be selling the cigarette sticks to little kids. Cancer wasn't really on the mind of anybody, but most thought smoking was an expensive and dirty habit. That having been said, it wasn't dirty enough to stop most smoking and chewing, and the local tobacco crops had enough economic impact to subtly suggest that the candy sticks were part of supporting the local economy. Common sense eventually prevailed and candy cigarettes were removed from the shelves—about the same time their customers had graduated to the full array of real cigarettes that were dispensed from the metal rack behind the counter.

Behind the check out counter, on the center shelf, below the cigarette and chewing tobacco products, was the candy bar shelf. This was the popular scene about 3:30 in the afternoon when the school bus dropped off several high school students. They hit the candy bar rack immediately after extracting a ten cent bottle of pop (the country term for soda) from the back room refrigerator. The popular candy bars such as Baby Ruth, Butterfinger, Three Musketeers, Milky Way, and the like, were supplemented by some itinerant bars that ran the course of a couple orders from Click Distributing before we gave up on their ability to compete with the old reliables. Only two brands of chewing gum made the shelf – Dentyne and the standard Wrigley's three: Spearmint, Doublemint and Juicy Fruit, the latter being the kid favorite. During season, bubble-gum stuffed packages of baseball cards were on the shelf, tantalizingly close to the somewhat taboo baseball cards that might accompany the Red Man chewing tobacco on the shelf above.

Another location of a candy was Uncle Alfred's private stash in a large drawer beneath the cash register. The candy wasn't always there, but it occasionally rested among the box of paper match books that were distributed with cigarettes, and other miscellaneous junk, including shotgun and .22 caliber shells. It wasn't exactly capricious, but it certainly wasn't predictable to whom or when he would give the candy, other than the certainty that it wasn't to adults or big kids. Adults had free coffee and cookies, and the big kids could pretty much fend for themselves by purchasing a candy bar. Sometimes there was a chagrined parent who felt the sugary treat inappropriate for junior, but never was this questioned as low level marketing ploy. It was really the gentle old Santa Claus effect, combined with some partial reinforcement theory, that kept that big brown drawer a mystery and hovering spot for the smallest of customers.

And it was the candy counter that brought home two harsh realties of this world for me – cavities and consumer debt. I noted as a small child that many customers would simply say "charge it," and walk out the door with their wares. And my family was no exception. Paying cash for everything we took up the stairs to our penthouse apartment five or six times a day would have been less than practical. So it was an easy ploy, when I wanted a penny sucker or some other treat, to tell my mother that we could just charge it. And unfortunately, at least for my teeth, she too often relented. But it was here that I came to seriously ponder the woes of financial indebtedness, and would worry that we might never have enough money to pay the eight pages of current purchases on the charge book that bore the name of Lee Felde, not to mention the huge stack of tallied sheets that were held inside the McCaskey.

I was not totally naïve to our personal finances, and probably correct in the assumption that our family didn't have much money. I do recall a time or two when I thought all the bills had been paid (or at least a $100 payment had been subtracted from the last entry of bills). But they always returned. So it was with my sense of obligation to struggling parents, combined with Lutheran guilt; and observations of good customers paying their bills and the bad ones who didn't return after insurmountable debt, that I was motivated to do something about the stack of bills. After an afternoon of serious contemplation, it was in a dramatic and staged scene in front of the candy counter (the source of my sins) that I presented to my mother a one-dollar bill to contribute to the cause. In retrospect, I think the staging in front of the counter was something conjured up in my subconscious Lutheran adolescent brain to roughly parallel confessional scenes I had seen on television murder mysteries. It was a major developmental stage in my life, and might have been even more so had my mother not been slightly dismissive (but nonetheless moved) since she knew the bigger picture of our family commune; a somewhat dysfunctional cooperative that sort of kept records, but ultimately shared what was needed, did what work was required and plugged along to pay the bills and keep the store going.

Since we had difficulty with our own internal family accounting and debt, it is no surprise that we weren't particularly good at managing our credit business in the store.

A lot of product inventory left the store without financial compensation. Accordingly, it was good the store didn't get credit from anyone else in attempts to enhance our business enterprise. Maybe it is more accurate to say it was good we had enough sense not to ask. Nobody would have seen it as a wise investment, except maybe a sucker like me who would have pitched in a dollar.

100th Anniversary

Chapter 8
Tobacco

Conjuring up images of a slow chugging railroad loco-
motive, or perhaps a circus calliope, the large black steam
engine tractor (about two or three times the size of normal
farm tractors) lumbered up the gravel road from the valley
in early spring, periodically blasting a shrill whistle or toot
to announce its presence and proclaim its role in commenc-
ing tobacco season in West Prairie. Large flat metal wheels
with protruding cross strips dug harmlessly into the gravel
roads but left significant impressions on the blacktop pave-
ment as it traversed from farm to farm. The conscientious
operator might have somehow removed the traction strips
to save the roads. But that was not necessarily the norm
and there was an unwritten code that this damage was a
community cost of doing business when once a year the
damaging intrusion was readily ignored by those who might
have had some responsibility for road repair.

In earlier years these practically stationary tractors
were used for heavy duty tasks that demanded large pulley
systems to power another implement such as a threshing
machine. Few of these mechanical throwbacks to another
farming era remained by the mid century, but those that
did were called into service to begin the tobacco growing
enterprise. These steam engines were rigged on the under-
side with large metal plates, about sixteen feet long, six feet

wide, and six inches deep – to deliver long sterilizing blasts of steam onto the ground for the purpose of killing any potential weed, seed or bacteria in the rich black soil that had been selected to serve as a "tobacco bed."

The tobacco beds, conforming to width of the steamed ground, were about six feet wide, and usually laid out in parallel strips, with a total of twenty or thirty yards of beds. Six inch high boards were dug into the ground, and provided the sides for the beds, as well as support for the thin white cheesecloth type fabric that constituted the "bed covers." Soon after sowing a thick layer of seeds, the beds were richly blanketed with thin and tightly packed plants about four inches tall, pressing the tops of beds and ready for transplant. The covers served to protect delicate plants by diffusing the bright rays of the sun and shelter them from heavy rain. Beds were carefully watered and tended. It was a good time for all but the most mellow and aged farm dogs to be tied up or kenneled, and on occasion there was horror story of cows getting out and trampling a tobacco bed.

This region of southwestern Wisconsin was blessed with a perfect geographic and climatic match that made it one of the few locations in the northern United States capable of producing a tobacco crop that could match and even surpass southern tobacco varieties. The rich dark soil, often sown to rye grass in the fall or spring to stabilize and enrich the ground, was plowed and dragged to a fine and smooth texture in the late spring and early summer, ready for planting by the first of June.

The transplanting of tobacco plants, termed "setting" was a multi-stage process that began with watering the plants in the beds so they could easily be extracted, but not watered so much as to create a muddy mess for the next step. They were pulled out individually, and when a handful was accumulated, they were placed in cardboard boxes, wooden bushel baskets or iron tubs; and then placed in the shade, waiting transport to a staging area next to the tobacco field. Almost anyone could pick the plants, but the job was best suited for those who had long enough arms to reach the center of the beds, and enough flexibility to continuously sit sideways, and balance precariously on the narrow edge of the bed or on plank that had been placed across the bed. A bed was picked multiple times, and could be re-picked when smaller plants began to fill in within a couple days; so care was taken to judiciously pick only the right size plants, and not "strip the beds." It wasn't really hard work, but required patience and the ability to twist and reposition the body. I enjoyed the first fifteen minutes, and basically was able to tolerate the painful contortion because I didn't want to embarrass myself in front of the elders and neighbor women who seemed more resiliently adapted to this job than impatient youth. The best temporary escape was volunteering to carry the plant boxes or water the beds to facilitate easy picking. But the tedious and back wrenching process provided the opportunity to visit in side-by-side fellowship, where the conversation was pleasant and rambling, and included the farm host, neighbors, passers-by and hired help. Since not every farm had a tobacco bed with plants it was not unusual to procure, often without cost, plants from neighboring farms.

Setting the tobacco required a small tractor that would pull the most diminutive of farm equipment – a transplanter, simply known as "the planter." The planter had two seats, occupied by a pair of "setters" with coordinated timing and good finger dexterity. A neighbor high school student, Linda, and my brother Dave were the most stable occupants of the planter for Alfred's field. They would carefully pick off single plants from a large metal box in front of their seats, and alternately insert them into constricting rubber sleeves that rotated in Ferris wheel fashion that eventually, and gently, carried and deposited the plants into the ground, accompanied by a dose of water from a drum that was also affixed to the planter. Good setters could often accomplish the rhythmic task without error or missing a plant for multiple rows; but, on occasion plants would stick together or the quiet focus and conversation would erupt into giggles and laughter. At such times, the driver, Alfred, whose job it was to keep perfectly even rows, and couldn't afford time to turn around, could only surmise the state of comical affairs behind him and would join in the fun and gently cajole the duo. Usually a younger child, in this case me, would be following the planter with a handful of plants and a small bucket of water, to poke a hole in the ground, douse it with water, and carefully insert a replacement for the plants missed by the distracted setters.

Uncle Alfred's field, where I spent most of my tobacco working time, was always supplied with plants from elsewhere, generally from two or three sites. Consequently our crop was often the last to be set. But the intense growing season allowed planting as late as early July, when the final setting of plants in Uncle Alfred's tobacco field would be celebrated at the store front with root beer floats, firecrackers, and a miniature Independence Day fireworks display. Within a few weeks, the elation of a completed planting gave way to the more individual and boring effort of hand hoeing and weeding to supplant cultivation with a small tractor. It wasn't fun, and carried the danger of an ill placed whack with the hoe that would sever the tender plant base. Such transgression was best disguised by a temporary dirt prop and ignored, with the mysterious plant death left to be noticed a few days later if someone happened to be so observant.

August brought with it the preparations for harvest. "Topping" the plant occurred when the plants had grown about waist high, nearly full size. The top narrow stem of the plant was snapped off just above the large leaves, with the intended result of the grocery bag sized leaves broadening and filling out even more. After walking about thirty yards into the field, the oil from the edges of the tobacco leaves began to be noticed as a sticky substance on the topper's jeans and lower shirttails. Strong hands and wrists were required to leverage a quick snap on the inch thick stems. Topping and walking through the green field also called for vigilance to spot the camouflaged tobacco worm, a thick fat creature that resembled a short decorated green cigar with antennae. Though the camouflage was good, three inch holes in the leaves generally signaled their nearby presence. Upon destruction under foot, the green slime left no doubt about its diet. Although younger children may not have been able to snap off the tough plant tops, they could easily join in this stage of the harvest by search and destroy missions for the green nemesis. While instant squashing of the worm may have been satisfying, it was not unusual to collect them in coffee cans to validate their efforts, or perhaps even collect a minor bounty for a full can. And the ultimate challenge from peers, occasionally accepted (but only once), was to bite the nasty creature in two.

Mother Nature responded to the topping process by producing a series of small shoots or "suckers" that emerged from the broken stem. And so within a week or two, and just prior to harvest, the suckers needed to be removed in the same manner and for much the same purpose as topping the plant. But additionally, the removal of the suckers assured a uniform drying and curing of the plant after harvest. Suckering was even more arduous than topping the plant, since there were multiple suckers, and although smaller than the original plant top, they often were stubbornly tough and resistant to the crisp snapping technique used in topping.

One of the few labor saving innovations that emerged during this era of tobacco production was the development of a chemical to prevent the suckers from growing after the topping process. The chemical name is far too long to record, but generically known as a "plant growth inhibitor" with warning labels that even shocked us at a time when 2-4-d was liberally used to eradicate weeds and, inadvertently, eagles. Affectionately this product was referred to as "sucker dope" and one gallon cans were mixed with water in hand held metal canisters with attached spraying devices, and applied immediately after topping. We used a moderate amount of care as we applied the solution to the top leaves of the tobacco plant to avoid inhaling the fine mist, and most of us probably escaped harm, but one can only imagine the marriage of that product with the carcinogenic leaves.

And the harvest time began—a time shared by neighbors, the schools and county. County schools opened later than others to accommodate farm families who needed their children to engage in the harvest. The Vernon County Fair, proudly advertised as the last fair in the state, held off until mid September to be sure the rural community was all available, and the tobacco could be proudly included in the exhibition halls.

Getting a harvest crew was essential, since the labor intensive product needed many bodies to accomplish the multiple, skilled, and time dependent tasks in a short time. The crews varied, depending on family size, but generally involved neighbors in exchange work, some hired friends and neighbors with experience in tobacco, and those semi-retired farmers who found the work enjoyable and relished the fellowship of the field.

The first step involved several men, each chopping his way down a row of tobacco, gently laying each plant to the ground. This was accomplished with a tobacco axe, a short axe with a thin square steel blade at the end. Files were frequently pulled from overalls to sharpen the axes, and ensure that one swift whack would sever the thick base of the plant. After a designated corner of the field was laid flat, the crew might be joined by others, particularly children who could engage in the next step of piling the plants. Timing was important in this step because insufficient wilt would result in plants being crisp and damaged in handling; plants left too long in the sun would begin to burn, dry out and become brittle. After the sun and heat provided a sufficient wilt for the cut plant, workers could now carefully grab two or three plants in each hand and methodically create a pile of plants, with the end of the stalks neatly formed as a point for the spearing operation.

Spearing seemed to be reserved for the old time pros of the tobacco industry, and an ideal task for a skilled senior worker who might not manage the heavy work as well as the younger laborer. But it was a skilled task, where errors caused frustrating delays and damaged plants, since an ill speared plant could fall from the lath in later handling. The spearers would bring a "tobacco jack," an unusual large wooden, irregular tripod type device, near the pile of plants, and insert the end of a four foot long lath into a slot that held the lath waist high and parallel to the ground. A small hollow metal spear (the pros always carried their own personal spear) was then placed over the other end of the lath, facing the pile. Then about five or six plants were individually speared, several inches from the stalk base, and slid to an even distribution on the lath. Plants that were speared too high, or off center, would result in split plants. And the distinct sound of a snapping lath, generally accompanied by under the breath expressions of disgust, indicated a less than perfectly orchestrated jab of the plant on a lath. Plants from the broken lath were removed and gently re-speared.

The full lath was then laid flat on the ground in piles, ready for pick up.

At any time in the operation, if the sun was too direct, the top plants on a pile of speared or un-speared tobacco might be flipped over to prevent burning. And at any other time in the process, when each step of the process was at a logical break point, there would be mid field refreshments and fellowship, both morning and afternoon. Coffee, soft drinks and water accompanied cookies, donuts, and luncheon meat sandwiches. Coffee was acceptable in any weather, and the old bachelor farmer might be inclined in the middle of a sweltering 90+ degree afternoon to suggest that the hot coffee served to drive the heat out of a person. And it was a *good* time, not unlike late night discussions and debates in the store. It may have gotten a bit livelier than in the store, with the outdoor environment ripe for pranks. On one such occasion, with most of the crew in cahoots with crew chief Alfred, the heart of Tommy's bologna sandwich had been replaced with a carefully cut piece of red rubber inner tube. Recounting the prank with laughter 50 years later suggests it was successful.

The layers of speared and stacked tobacco were picked up by crews who loaded them flat on wagons or, better for the plant leaves, on tobacco racks. Tobacco racks were specially designed wagons, with two elevated parallel wooden bars, that could accommodate the exact width of the tobacco lath – the ends of the lath each perched on the bars, with the tobacco plants hanging straight down. The loaded racks were then driven to the tobacco shed. From a distance the tobacco shed appeared to be a huge barn with no unusual characteristics other than stately size. But closer inspection revealed that the long side boards on the barn were affixed with hinges for the purpose of airing out the tobacco, or closing out the outside cold or moisture that would come in the next several months.

The inside of the barn was equally unique and was the only part of the harvest where a distinct labor inequality existed. Only the strongest, fittest, and dexterous of the workers belonged on the series of long parallel poles that ran through the barn where the lath would be hung, much like on the tobacco rack, as the first step in the drying process. The difference was that in the barn, there were multiple layers of these pole systems. Incredible strength was required as one person lifted a lath high above his head to the outstretched hand of his co-worker, who was leaning over with outstretched hand below his feet that were balanced on the barn poles. And this process was then repeated as the middle-man handed lath to the worker above who would hang the peak of the shed. It took a minimum of three workers to hang the highest levels, depending on the shed configuration, the ability of the weakest human link, and the height of the barn. Those who hung the peak were the most likely to be paid for their work; and if other workers were paid, they were clearly on a lower pay scale than those who risked life and limb in the barn. Typically they were young, strong, and perhaps less connected with the family and community nature of the harvest. While they may have been friends, they were clearly high skilled and hired help.

Bad judgment leads to danger on the farm. In the case of tobacco shed indiscretions, there were abundant warnings and stories of poles that were unsecured on their support beams. It was also bad decision making to utilize a tobacco shed as a machinery storage facility while men were balancing on the poles above; a misstep could mean impalement on a variety of metal objects. It remains to be seen what influenced Alfred's questionable judgment: lack of sufficient crew on a given day, misperception and denial of danger, or a male ego attempting to prove itself to others while challenging the laws of nature. In this case, the obvious law of nature should have been: *Short and Fat Doesn't Balance Well on Poles*. There must have been something coordinated, or at least balanced, in his fall, since he negotiated a perfectly timed and equal landing – on both heels!

His close friend Earl, an accomplished plumber and tobacco farmer, aided in Alfred's convalescence by constructing an iron pipe orthopedic support system in the upstairs of the Halverson family farmhouse. It must have been a humbling experience to still be in that mammoth pipe contraption months later at Christmas time, with both broken heels still pointing toward the ceiling. Added to the frustrations of being an invalid was having to delegate to others his treasured Christmas ritual, and store responsibility —sorting and distributing lutefisk to friends and customers. His only role was to get reports of the activities, and from his bed, smell and pass judgment on the quality of fish being prepared in his house as the smells wafted up the stairs to his bedroom. And that year it smelled bad.

For Alfred, it was probably some minor consolation at Christmas time to receive final reports of the last stage of the tobacco harvest, and perhaps even a paycheck from the "tobacco pool" cooperative. About Thanksgiving time of each year tobacco farmers looked for weather defined as "case weather," a spell of weather when fog and humidity crept into the tobacco sheds to renew a soft, supple, and leathery feel to the now brown leaves that just days earlier had been dry and brittle. The smell in the barn was rich, similar to a good cigar before burning, but capturing an intoxicating freshness from thousands of plant aromas as they mingled with the cool, damp air. At this point the tobacco could be taken down from the poles without crumbling the leaves, placed on wagons and transported to barns, garages, or small heated buildings that (at least seasonally) were affectionately referred to as "strip shanties." In these locations the old seasoned pros of tobacco gathered to methodically strip the leaves off the tobacco stalk and place the leaves, handful by handful, into a paper lined box. When the box was filled, the tobacco was tightly wrapped in the paper to form a bale weighing about forty pounds, tied with twine, and piled neatly, finally ready to leave the farm.

Stripping the tobacco was a quiet, relaxed process that might have strung out over several weeks. There wasn't an urgency to beat the weather, and the conversations of the mature, or retired, tobacco veterans recalled crops of years gone by, the latest discussion on tobacco molds (influenced by high levels of case in the leaves), or whatever manly gossip and jokes were fitting for the particular day. The biggest debates might have occurred over the amount of coal and fuel oil in the stoves that heated the small areas, and where the particular strippers were located—to bask, perhaps bake, in the heat of a nearby stove, or to be more comfortable five yards away, but with a twinge of cold creeping to one's feet through the bare floor.

And so it was – a crop that gathered community, allowed for fellowship, and provided supplemental income to the dairy farmers. It had tremendous economic impact for some. The story is told of brothers who planted a field of corn, only to have it totally destroyed by cutworms. In despair and desperation, they plowed the field under and planted a late crop—seventeen acres of tobacco; and reportedly they paid off the farm that year. Tobacco paid off the debt on many farms in post depression years.

More than other crops, it was a community venture of sharing and exchange work. Empathic neighbors appeared when weather threatened to damage a crop during harvest. It was a crop that was very labor intensive, required a variety of skills, with teams working together. And it remained immune to the intrusions of oversized, loud, isolating, and labor saving machinery that was beginning to transform other aspects of the farming industry. It was a process that involved and honored the work of young and old, and facilitated conversation between neighbors and generations.

Although the research about tobacco and cancer came in later years, it was still obvious to most that tobacco was a dirty crop, or a least that smoking tobacco was a dirty habit. So there were rationalizations about growing tobacco. The minister's wife, who lived next door, and had sons who were known as excellent tobacco hands, liked to say that some of the tobacco product was used as an insecticide. Whether or not this was true—or if it was a twisted tale related to the fact that a good cigar was the best mosquito repellent when night fishing on the banks of the Mississippi—didn't really matter; it was still a rationalization. Another rationalization in the category of "lesser evils," was that cigar smoking wasn't as bad a habit as cigarette smoking. Many took pride in the fact that the local broad leaf tobacco was historically used for high quality cigar wrappings, associated with fine Cuban tobacco. But eventually, even the fine local crops wound up being homogenized, ground up and thrown into some unknown hopper of tobacco parts, and used for chewing tobacco.

But even in later years when only those in total denial could refute the connection to cancer, tobacco remained a crop of mysterious pride. Although I hate the effects and devastation caused by tobacco, I find myself somehow proud as I recount the stories of raising tobacco. My father, who was one of the gentlest men of the farming community and never would have considered doing anyone harm by raising a dangerous crop, still, in his later and dying years recounted with great pride a particular crop he raised that paid for a new car during the World War II years. It was a pride I never saw related to the ostensibly virtuous dairy farming that absolutely dictated his schedule, ruined his body and took years of enjoyment from his life.

There are other perspectives of tobacco farming. In his book, *The Land Remembers,* about growing up on a dairy farm in southwest Wisconsin, Ben Logan talks about tobacco as being a crop that gave nothing back and only served to take from the land and the people who were slaves to the process of raising it. I can't speak to the agricultural technicalities, but I know that tobacco was much more than a crop and a supplemental income. At least in West Prairie, it provided a glimpse into what a community and agriculture might aspire to. It would be easy to be romantic about it all if it didn't kill people.

***

Tobacco was introduced into Vernon County in 1870, and as much as 7000 acres was in production in the 1940's. But for years, even back to the 1960's, tobacco had been regulated, and annual acreage allotments were on the decline. In 2005 Vernon County Wisconsin finally ended its long affair with tobacco, with one four acre field remaining and reportedly no place to market the product. 2004 was the last season of production for virtually all farmers. Combined with diminished access to market centers, farmers had little choice but to accept the lucrative offers from the United States Tobacco Buyout Program. The local newspaper, the Vernon County Broadcaster (June 23, 2005) detailed the rich history and bittersweet endings of this historic and controversial crop.

Chapter 9
Salesmen

Swearing and bad language were simply not acceptable in my family. The worst I ever heard was a frustrated "jeepers" from my mother when a swarm of flies rushed through an open screen door from the upstairs porch. So it was a daring venture one morning, when, after I had been sitting behind the store counter waiting for something exciting to happen, that I ran through the back room of the store and up the seventeen steps to our penthouse apartment above the store. The direct stimulus to my run had been a flashy, Brylcreemed black haired salesman in a plaid shirt who had lunged through the front door of the store only seconds earlier.

Yes, imitation was a great way to test the boundaries of foul language, and if it was too objectionable, I could simply claim ignorance because I was mimicking the salesman. Just like the salesman, I made my dramatic entrance through the apartment door, and in a proud shout, exclaimed, "Cheez Whiz!" The flat reaction from my mother suggested that I would have been better served to sit around and discover what that guy had been selling, rather than assume he had disrespectfully crossed some forbidden language barrier. Cheez Whiz ultimately turned out to be a great seller, and I especially liked it on toast, despite the embarrassing flashback to my first encounter with the product.

The salesmen (there were never any women) came in all shapes and sizes, personalities and styles. Occasionally there would be one-timers floating through with a unique product. Aunt Ruth was a sucker for those guys and would wind up buying a box of some product (revolutionary glass cleaner?) that would never sell. She probably did it out of charity and a lack of assertiveness training. And I am sure she knew the product would never sell because my family always got the first free sample, which would have instantly wiped out any profits if, in fact, the product did sell. Usually it was a total loss. But she had the good sense to buy only one box.

Years of Faithful Shoe Sales

There were the irregulars, such as the glove and footwear salesmen, who would show up several times a year. The good ones, reinforcing their company credibility, would send a postcard a week in advance so we could inventory the need for three or five buckle boots; work, jersey, or canvas gloves, depending on the season. The annual appearance in May or June of the fireworks salesman was slightly unnerving. His demeanor suggested he might have been a displaced front desk clerk from a sleazy hotel in a Hitchcock movie. As his slight frame quietly slipped in the front door, in a barely audible voice, he would look over his shoulder and whisper an inquiry about our interest in the contraband that apparently originated out of state since Wisconsin didn't allow the sale of fireworks. We would never have thought of selling something illegal (except to maybe our closest friends) and Aunt Ruth made a quick exit at his appearance. But Uncle Alfred would occasionally get a few legal sparklers, topped of with a ten dollar secretive purchase of Roman Candles, which eventually found themselves strapped to the mailboxes across the street from the store for luminary delights on the 4th of July.

Something internal, never something said aloud, suggested to me that the candy salesmen were a bit lower on the traveling salesperson status ladder than the others such as the bread man (clearly the highest in my book). Maybe it was the limited sales volume, but it could have been the higher turnover rate of the candy vendors. Most of the names have gone by the wayside, but there was Tiny, who weighed at least 300 pounds. He was stereotypical jolly, but one suspected that beneath the surface he had the

capacity for toughness and stern demeanor that undoubtedly served him well in his next step – owning a tavern in
a nearby heavy drinking river town. One can only guess
how the transition from children's bad habits to those of
adults served his vocational dreams. Unable to articulate
such ponderings when I reached the legal drinking age and
visited his establishment, I simply settled for a cordial hello
and a bottle of Budweiser. I am guessing the memory of me
as freckled little red-haired kid behind the candy counter
wasn't as vivid as mine of his 300 pound frame, so he didn't
approach the topic either.

Although most salesmen were fairly long term in their
jobs, some were transferred, some found little satisfaction
in the routine, and others were problems waiting to happen.
One such memorable character was a short term milkman
who needed access to the semi- private back room of the
store. Strangers never got to go back there, but friends
did. It housed multiple refrigerators, where the sodas, milk,
cheese and meat were stored. Usually the "milk refrigerator" could be viewed from the front room of the store
since it was directly adjacent to the door that usually was
left open when customers or those clerking accessed the
products. But this particular milkman seemed to like the
backroom door closed as he stocked the refrigerator and it
wasn't long before suspicions arose. The backroom served
as product storage, but also was the random repository
for multiple tools that served Uncle Alfred in his plumbing
and electrical trades. Not to be outsmarted by the suspected thief, Alfred and my father devised a plan to spy
on his secretive refrigerator stocking. Another door in the

middle of the back room opened to stairs that descended to the basement. They carefully neatened up (no small task) a table that sat close to that door and held mostly cartons of soda before it melded into general purpose and junk storage. Planted on a cleared spot was small pair of pliers, strategically placed to be viewed through the hole they had drilled through the basement door.

And of course they succeeded in observing the miscreant as he deftly slipped the pliers into his pocket. Why they never did anything about it is a mystery. It may have been that they wanted to avoid conflict, embarrassment or getting him into trouble – all pretty standard Scandinavian traits my family seemed to inherit. Or maybe, and I would like to think this is the case, they just hadn't gotten around to judiciously deciding what was best to do (except closely monitor future visits) by the time he was no longer a delivery man, which happened in the next two weeks. Conversations with his successor suggested that this behavior probably accompanied him elsewhere.

There were others who sort of fit into the salesmen genre, even though they didn't sell anything. They still stopped at the store for business reasons (or at least used that as an excuse to stop), made friends, and drank plenty of coffee.

I always felt sorry for the United Parcel Service men, dressed in their dark, heavy brown uniforms. They were in a constant hurry, hot and sweaty in the summer, looked stressed, and that stress was compounded by not knowing where to deliver their packages far out in the country. It was also long before cellular phones, so they would come into the store and ask to use the phone and inquire regarding directions to their drop-off addresses. They always appeared rushed when hospitality was offered; their message was that it was against UPS policy to do unauthorized stops. Consequently they guzzled the coffee, looking over their shoulders as if they were secret agents under surveillance. They burned their lips, and *never* sat at the coffee table. While there was sympathy for the men in brown whose positions prevented them from the norm of coffee and fellowship, it wasn't too deep, since they were rumored to be very well paid.

The mailmen were a distinct group, fairly stable since they had government jobs, and mostly respected because of the service they provided to everyone in the community. And over the years, they all managed to schedule their mail route through West Prairie and the store sometime within an hour of mid-day. Although the menu varied, most of the mailmen were served free lunches at the coffee table. Shortly before the arrival of the mailman, Aunt Ruth or Uncle Alfred would prepare a plate of something they were about to eat for lunch or, more often, go to the refrigerator in the back room. There they retrieved the lunch specialty, a long narrow roll of spicy Farley's summer sausage, brought it back to the meat slicer, and cut four or five slices that fell on a piece of wax paper. With some good fortune the slicer would disrupt the casing so it would fall off each slice without the need to handle the freshly sliced meat. The carefully tended slices were then placed on the coffee counter next to a box of saltines that had just been pulled off the rack of cookies and crackers that was conveniently located next to the coffee table. And, of course, they set out a clean coffee cup.

And the crossroads, besides providing the approximate line of school district boundaries, was the dividing line of postal routes. So it was not unusual for the Viroqua mailman to encounter the DeSoto route person at the coffee table. While the store and our family primarily identified with the Viroqua address, the optional DeSoto address seemed to be the choice of Uncle Alfred, particularly for business use. My guess is that the DeSoto address, originating from the river town of DeSoto, conjured up historical roots associated with past days of commerce—river traffic and trains that found DeSoto as a stopping point before they headed north to the businesses of LaCrosse and eventually, Minnesota.

The free meal service for some of the regulars, what was served, and how, was just one example of the blurred boundaries of what was for sale, what was for give-away, and what was personal possession within the confines of the store. Observant strangers who inquired would be told that we didn't serve or sell lunches, but they experienced free coffee, and were often embarrassed by wanting to purchase some personal item that was stored, or just carelessly left sitting on the store shelves. A first time visitor would have been confused attempting to sort out who were the salesmen, proprietors and customers. Customers helped themselves to coffee, served the salesmen, and prepared their own bills. The proprietors needed to be prompted to wait on customers who wanted service, and the sale sometimes felt like an intrusion on more important matters.

Bread man, meat man, candy man, potato chip man, milkman, dry cleaner man – they all took something with them. They accepted payment in cash and counter-signed checks. They took friendships and tales of the rural life to their city families. One was a thief and took a pair of pliers. Most of them left with the satisfaction of coffee and cookies. The best were mobile counselors whose warmth and anonymity allowed them to absorb the frustrations of the proprietors or the griefs of the community, pack them with their wares into the big box delivery truck, and return the following week to engage in another exchange of goods and unexpected services.

And they all left something beyond their merchandise. Some left information about life beyond the country. There were stories of vacations or hobbies. Some confided about their families and sorrows; or shared a joke, a bit of laughter, and some armchair philosophy. To some, and they were generally the short lived salesmen, the store was only a stop on the way to someplace else. They never were able to pause, either driven by themselves, or their company. They left the impression of a hurried world. But perhaps the biggest gift, shared and left, was the gift of time. Some of the special friends and confidants awoke an hour earlier in the day than needed in order to share in our coffee centered community. Some delayed their arrival home, even after long hours and extended miles, for a few minutes of fellowship at the counter. Relationships grow in many ways. But the intentional gift of extra time from our transient friends nurtured improbable bonds and stretched our world in subtle and sometimes far reaching ways.

Chapter 10
Fighting Communists

My mother summarized the well ingrained public mindset of the 1950's about communists – "they could be sitting right next to you in church." And the post Korean War thinking was that the Soviets could launch a nuclear air attack via the North Pole. Radio advertising from the Air Force suggested the possibility of such invasions:

> It may not be a very cheerful thought but the Reds right now have about a thousand bombers that are quite capable of destroying at least 89 American cities in one raid...Won't you help protect your country, your town, your children? Call your local Civil Defense Office and join the Ground Observer Corps today. (1)

West Prairie was ready to sign on for such a patriotic response. My aunt, Aleda Halverson, having served as a Navy nurse in New Guinea and the Pacific during World War II, was the logical person with the patriotic, military and organizational background to become the first local coordinator of the Ground Observer Corps. With the store as the gathering point of the community, and no specific site or watchtower available, the Halverson family home across the road from the store was generously offered as an observation post. The attic of the homestead provided access to a small 8ft. x 8 ft. observation platform, with wrought iron ornamental railing, on the house roof. The attic included an old crank style telephone; detailed instructions were posted on the wall for the volunteer observers to ring Viroqua and call for the Minneapolis Filter Center at pre-designated times, or when an aircraft was sighted:

> 1. *Call the Filter Center July 14th at 8:00 AM, 12:00 noon and 12:00 midnight*
> 2. *Call the Filer Center on July 15th and everyday thereafter at 12:00 noon and 12:00 midnight*
>
> *Ring Viroqua and call for the Minneapolis Filter Center, Then say "Observation Post, Peter, Peter, 5-2 Area reporting."*
>
> 3. *Report all aircraft sighted to the Filter Center.*
> 4. *Aircraft Flash?? Reports delayed longer than 6 minutes will not be reported* (2)

Observers would come in pairs when the Air Defense Command issued an alert. They entered the house through the kitchen, wound around corners past the pantry, by-passed the dining room, and found themselves in the parlor at the base of the stairs. Undoubtedly many paused at the base of the winding, deep maple-stained staircase to view the railing directly above. And then made the visual connection of that railing, from which my Aunt Inga had fallen when she was a small girl, to the two deep teeth marks that marked the corner of the bottom step. They acknowledged that her survival, save for two loose teeth, was a miracle, while they climbed to the landing where they peered out at the garage and windmill, and then took the next flight to the upstairs hallway.

Halverson Family Farmhouse

There were four bedrooms upstairs, a door to the attic stairs, plus a bathroom that was well appreciated after long hours of cool air and hot coffee on the observation deck. My confused, dying grandmother rested in the bedroom nearest the attic stairs. She was attended to regularly by her family, and me, at the age of four, in my white nursing uniform that had been supplied by my aunts Inga and Aleda, both professional nurses. There are no accounts of her confusion related to my childhood gender bending of job roles and attire, but she is well remembered as asking, "Who are all those people, and why are they coming and going through my house?" It was probably a pretty good question.

Snoopy House

Eventually, about the time my grandmother died, do-
nations and volunteer labor enabled the construction of a
small hut atop a prominent mound on the Dregne farm,
visible from the West Prairie Store, about one mile (as the
crow flies) to the southeast. It was complete with a telephone installed by the Vernon Telephone Co-op, and intended to replace the intimacies of the Halverson observation deck. It resembled a large doghouse. But the Red Scare
was beginning to wane, Wisconsin Senator Joseph McCarty
was censured, and radar systems were advancing. Beyond
that, it is hard to imagine that enthusiasm would have survived long, in the middle of a desolate field, far away from
friendship, a warm house and coffee pot. The building was
never occupied, except:

> Some years ago, Snoopy the famed cartoon character,
> like the famed World War I Ace he is depicted to be in

the Peanuts cartoon, suddenly appeared in his make-
believe airplane on top of the little house. Now after 40
years, Snoopy has flown away, but the little house on the
mound along with a Certificate of Recognition for Volun-
teer Services in support of the Air Defense of the United
States, dated 19 June, 1957, the Wings of an Observer
lapel pin, and the memories of the volunteers remain—
mementos of a community's spirit and patriotism. (3)

***

There were more practical ways to fight communism, and the most obvious way was to promote participation in the electoral process. Elections and other voting in the Sterling Township took place at the Town Hall, several hundred yards to the east of the store. The 1960's version of the Town Hall, that also functioned as a 4-H meeting center, was itself a reflection of changing times – an abandoned rural school building, a by-product of school consolidations, that was transported via semi-trailer moving crews to its new West Prairie home.

Church and state came together in West Prairie in a creative manner when the North West Prairie Lutheran Church women served lunch in the store on election days. It was a healthy (except for the food), patriotic venture that embraced the core values of rural America. The wooden counter that fronted the gloves and shoes was perfectly cleared, along with the adjacent glass counter and display case. Atop the counters were rows of assorted slices of pie, which could be purchased with a generous scoop of ice-cream. Coffee and milk were the standard beverages, and soft drinks could be purchased from the store. The main lunch course, served up on plain white Sunbeam hamburger buns, was affectionately labeled a "bar-b-que" on a large sheet of white tag board. In reality, the sandwich was a sloppy-joe concoction that featured ground hamburger and a healthy mixture of chicken gumbo soup. At some level, this was even considered a secret recipe since, unlike the pies and cakes, only a select group provided the main course. Nobody every questioned that this wasn't barbeque, at least in the traditional sense. I never remember barbeque sauce on the store shelves, or being part of the simple hot dog, hamburger or steak grilling efforts of the prairie. West Prairie just wasn't that far west.

***

Three themes highlighted the Nixon/Kennedy presidential campaign of 1960, at least in the minds of the Tewalt grade school students. The first, underlying theme was the continued threat of communism and concern for security. The second was Republican vs. Democrat. And the third theme was the nationwide debate about the propriety of a Catholic in the White House. In reality, the communism threat and security didn't register much with the grade school kids, and it would be surprising if any of us really were significantly aware of the Cuban Missile Crisis in 1962 shortly after Kennedy's election. So the communism threat was amorphously wrapped into the debate of which political party was the best. And the best political party, at least in the mind of grade schoolers (years before they switched parties in college), was the party of their parents' choosing. Of course the Republican kids didn't have any problems tossing out the inference that we shouldn't have a Catholic in the White House, since that would only lead to papal dominance. One couldn't help but feel sorry for the one outspoken student whose parents were in the distinct Democratic minority of the West Prairie community. His retort, about the only one he could muster in the terrain of religious bigotry, regretfully, was more of the same: "Well, by rights Nixon shouldn't be president either, since he's a Quaker." And I don't remember the one Catholic kid saying anything.

***

1) Shaffel, Kenneth. <u>The Emerging Shield: The Air Force and the Evolution of Continental Air Defense, 1945-1960</u>, pp. 158-159. University Press of the Pacific, 2004.

2) Notice posted in the attic of the Halverson farmhouse.

3) Skildum, Keith, article submitted to <u>Vernon County Heritage, 150th Anniversary, 1844-1994.</u>

Thank you to Mr. Skildum for his background information on this chapter, as well as DeSoto High School students for their research on this topic for a WKBT, Channel 8, LaCrosse news report, July 7, 2001.

Chapter 11
Tewalt School

One mile to the east of the store, nestled in a small valley on the prairie was the Tewalt School building that had served the community for decades. As the country stores were unlike city retailers, the rural schools operated in marked contrast to city education, and also like the country stores, were in a period of transition – in fact, this era brought about the end of an American institution in many communities.

The morning routine that originated at the store, except for the warm fall or spring days when bicycles might be used, had Uncle Alfred loading my brother and me into the latest version of his relatively "hot" Chevy, drive past the West Prairie Cheese Factory, stop at the neighbors to pick up one or two more passengers, drive down the road to the curve in Highway 82 that accentuated the presence of the North West Prairie Lutheran Church, and then descend down the quarter mile Tewalt Hill. There, at the T-junction with a gravel road, was the large, square red brick schoolhouse, complete with a canopied bell tower. A large swing set, merry-go-round and small grass play area rested between the building and a row of large pine trees that defined the west border of the school ground with a neighbor's cow pasture. The front door of the school faced north to the highway; immediately behind the school, the landscape quickly sloped to an acre of rich farmland affectionately referred to as the "flat," that served as a multipurpose space for football, softball, and a variety of winter games.

Students gathered in the school basement, cloakroom, or playground to await the summons of the bell, but the farming community schedules didn't allow for many students to be hanging around the building early. After the bell ringing all the students joined in the Pledge of Allegiance, and two students took the carefully folded flag outside the building to raise it up the flagpole. The same students would retrieve the flag at day's end, fold it in the sanctioned manner and return it to the classroom.

The school population was generally about 25-30 students, fairly well dispersed among the eight grades; plus the teacher and the part time cook, Mrs. Cunningham. The class day began as the teacher methodically called separate age and subject groups to tables adjacent to his/her desk at the front of the classroom and proceeded to discuss and review the material individually or via blackboard sessions. And frequently the class would take its turn at the board to publicly display cognition of the language, spelling or math lessons. The ultimate effect was a public accountability of student learning, but it also reinforced the other students who had already passed through that particular lesson before. For those who hadn't progressed to the level being addressed at the front of the room, it was an advanced organizer – the early and unrecognized rendition of accelerated learning programs. And at times when students freely walked about the room to work at tables and displays, the older students mentored the younger ones on their lessons or projects. Wandering aimlessly about the schoolroom wasn't acceptable, however, and unless on an assigned task, students would raise their hands with the appropriate number of fingers for a bathroom break or authorization to give or seek academic assistance from another student.

Of course the one room, one teacher, multi-grade setting had its challenges, and imposed demands that might be beyond the comprehension (and certification requirements) of today's teachers. One such challenge was addressing the arts in a manner that could accommodate eight grade levels as well as do so in a manner that allowed a measure of success for a teacher who might not have been skilled in multiple artistic veins. Our teachers attempted to meet the challenge, and their endeavors were often signaled in advance by Gary's presence at the school radio, that held a position of honor on a shelf in the front of the classroom. About 1:25 p.m. Gary would turn on the radio so the tubes could warm up, and as a quiet signal crackled, keeping the volume low with the intent of not disturbing others, he would lean his ear into the speaker and patiently roll the dial until he found Wisconsin Public Radio. Depending on the day, program offerings included *Let's Draw*, *Let's Sing*, or *Let's Read*—a series intended to engage the audience with either dramatic readings, sing-alongs with musical lessons and comments interspersed between songs, or specific instructions for a creative art project (which the teacher had already prepared for by means of a program guide and a tiny supplies budget). It was usually a step up for the youngest students, whose glue and cutting expertise had been limited to their *Puzzle Pages* workbook. Any way you looked at it — from unpredictable radio reception to rag-tag supplies for a diverse age group—the art projects were a venture of faith for the teacher.

Multiple arts and more; theatre, poetry, music, public speaking, and simply looking cute for parents came together in December for the annual Christmas program. Everyone participated except for a family whose particular church denomination didn't allow for celebratory events; but their acceptance of the holiday ritual of others and their efforts to contribute (like home-baked treats) were appreciated by even those not old enough to comprehend religious diversity. The mutual respect within the community never allowed this to become a scenario of isolation; at least that was the impression of the majority.

Christmas was the only time of the year when the teacher's patience was severely tested, as manifested by the annual frustrated and half screaming proclamation on the day before the show, "That's it, it will have to go on as it is!" It was honest frustration precipitated by the holiday excitement of children, all going in different directions of preparation and frivolity. And it also included a realistic fear that, despite weeks of practice, the lines were not adequately rehearsed, that the wooden stage in the front of the classroom might finally collapse after years of benign neglect, or that the makeshift muslin curtain that hung on fencing wire and held up by hooks in the wall, might come crashing down as the result of an ill placed body part. But the program always came off in grand fashion. The plays were appropriately funny and poignant at the right moments, the songs were ripe with the desired Christmas familiarity, and the little kids were attired it their holiday finest; and they were cute. Each family brought delicious holiday treats for the post program festivities, Christmas cookie crumbs found every corner of the school; parents, families, and the teacher mingled, enjoying the spirit of the season, and late in the evening everyone departed satisfied, entertained, exhausted, and ready for the Christmas break.

While the arts were sometimes a creatively addressed challenge, there never was any question about physical education. There simply wasn't need to carve out a curriculum slot since recess involved everyone in physical engagement. Recess always meant everyone, except those who had health concerns, going outside. But when rain forced everyone indoors, much to the chagrin of the teacher, new adventures emerged. If the teacher wasn't inclined to improvise with structured activities, students opted for dangerous games of tag in the concrete walled basement, or even softball and basketball as unheralded forerunners of arena sports. For softball participants the "crack of the bat" took on additional meaning as the clattering of bats dropped on the concrete floor echoed throughout the building. The term "catcher's box" also assumed new meaning as it was creatively positioned behind an open door, in a small recessed landing for the stairway that led to the student boot storage area and front door of the school. It remains a mystery how we escaped serious injury in this small concrete box that sported wire meshed basement windows to withstand flying footballs, softballs, basketballs and children.

Recess was a two-tiered structure with the "little kids" and "big kids" (the common term defining rights of passage and activities) getting slightly different allowances. The little kids got both morning and afternoon recesses; everyone got nearly an hour at noon, depending on how quickly lunch was consumed. But the record breaking recesses happened when the school district superintendent stopped by to visit the teacher. Actually, after a two hour lunch, we would begin to tire and guiltily wonder if something had mysteriously gone wrong within the school walls. Nothing unstructured like that would ever happen today, and if it did, there would certainly be a parent charging neglect of children and suggesting other misconduct.

Recess involved seasonal games of football and softball. The big kids played in the "flat" below the school, while the little kids generally occupied themselves with their own games on the upper play spaces, that is, unless the most talented in sports had been drafted to play ball with the big kids in the honored fields below. And in the spring the teacher would often succumb to the pleas of students to call a nearby country school and challenge them to a softball game. These turned into all school outings akin to family picnics; and fathers even generously volunteered their time in peak planting season to offer their umpiring services.

But winter sports reigned supreme in the recess department. Many of us stored wooden slat skis in the basement and simply went out the back door and glided down the slope to the flat. And almost everyone had sleds that, on a good day, could start at the far corner of the schoolyard and slide all the way around the school and wind up in the field below. The more adventurous trekked across the neighbor's fence, and walked several hundred yards to the "big hill' in the middle of his pasture. Naturally, these activities were not without danger, particularly since obstacles like trees and fence posts got in the way. On one occasion my friend wrapped his leg around a stump while sledding down the big hill, prompting me to run the several hundred yards back to the school, where I interrupted class to report the crisis. A couple of the big kids rushed to the hill and used long sleds as a gurney to transport Al back to the school, where his mother was waiting to take him to the hospital. He wore the horseshoe shaped row of stitches on his leg proudly. There was little need for a lecture on safety, and most of us figured out that rule number two (behind rule number one—not to run your sled into something) was to drag your legs directly behind your sled, rather than use them as side braking and turning mechanisms when doing slalom events among tree stumps.

Although much less often, the danger escalated when major snow or ice storms packed a solid sheet of a sledding pathway on Highway 82. Stern parental admonitions and a premature onset of good judgment kept me from such adventures, but a few fearless students climbed to the crest of the highway hill, pushed off, and gathered significant speed by the time they approached the schoolhouse corner and attempted to negotiate the right angle turn at the intersection. Some successfully made the turn, scraping their sled blades through to blacktop and then throwing gravel in the air as they entered the side road. Others survived the missed turn because they plummeted into big banks of the new snow, assuming they were fortunate enough to avoid the stop sign. The most successful of the sledding daredevils continued his affinity for speed in the high school years as he transported many of us in his car through the countryside at speeds that made even the most adventurous skittish. His favorite trick was to approach a corner at breakneck speed (like he did on his sled), only to go straight off onto a barely visible connecting road. He wasn't Catholic, so there wasn't a plastic Jesus on his dashboard, but in retrospect, I am convinced there was a guardian angel on board.

Winter games on the flat, such as snowball fights and the always popular "fox and geese" eventually gave way to spring. The exuberant spring spirits of school children and a short-lived phenomenon of the spring thaw fueled excitement over the opportunities provided by Mother Nature's seasonal transition. Melting snow flowed to the flat as the converging point of the small valley and the effect was an acre of knee high slush and water, flowing into the ditch and culvert that slowly deposited water to the woods on the other side of the road. It was a fantasyland for future engineers, as one well packed snow dam gave way to another. Sometimes the efforts were so successful that the water would back up enough to reach the road, rather than drain through the culvert, and at such times a rare adult intervention was needed to redirect activities. And the acre of slush was a magnificently huge puddle playground for students to slosh around in, provided we had sufficiently large and leak proof rubber boots (50% of the time, my boots were in such condition to require a boot liner of Sunbeam bread wrappers). One good sport of a teacher even decided to join in the spring slush wading ritual. Good intentions were countered by her weight distribution that limited dexterity in the wet muck. Her adventure ended when she became stuck and virtually immobile, fearing abandonment and a tortuous collapse into hypothermic disaster. Fortunately a couple of the big kids were summoned to help extract her from the slush and embarrassment. And they did.

We played together outside the school, and even rescued each other. Inside the school we took for granted that community responsibility was the norm and we learned how to use sweeping compound on the floors, regularly cleaned the blackboards, helped with kitchen duties, dealt with the trash, and even transported the ten gallon bucket of kitchen scraps to the ditch across the road. We were lectured in a group when we didn't play well together, and encouraged to help each other in diverse learning activities. We learned to respect the food that Mrs. Cunningham served, even if it was government surplus canned meat.

And on the treks home from school, as we dove off ten foot high snow banks, struggled to ride our bikes up the long hill, or laughed as my brother David fashioned discarded beer can clogs onto his shoes, we didn't think too much about what we had learned. Our parents got report cards with individual comments, and didn't pay too much attention, other than assuming we had learned something based on their intuitive impression of the teachers (and I never heard any bad comments about any of them). When district consolidation efforts closed the school in 1962, it didn't appear that anyone was thinking too much about what we had learned either. In fairness, maybe someone had some national research about the relative quality of rural schools, and perhaps some schools in the district had some deficiencies; but our graduates had proven themselves to be good students in high school, hard working soldiers and citizens, and often, successful college graduates.

Not surprising was the community reaction, which also focused on something other than measured learning. The core of protest and response was related to the loss of local control, and the loss of an institution that bound the community together. Uncle Alfred led the protest movement, and with a great deal of networking, and the unusual country action of seeking assistance from an attorney, he orchestrated the formation of the Tewalt Community Club. At the Tewalt School District meeting of May 1962, the board members voted to sell the school, land and fixtures to the Community Club for five dollars. It was an act of anger and in your face defiance, but it also spoke to a community desiring something – something of the past, something perhaps already lost.

There is a difference between "good ideas gone bad," and good ideas that don't work. The intent of the Community Club was to provide regular gatherings of fellowship, local entertainment; perhaps singing, games and potlucks. It was a vision not unlike church socials, but they were already a thing of the past and times were changing. Schools, like the store, were being influenced by declining rural populations and increased mobility.

Years later I was reminded of Uncle Alfred's dying dreams of the store, the school, and the Community Club when I ventured into an isolated, rustic log cabin tavern in the middle of a Pennsylvania forest. When I commented on the dearth of business to the elderly woman at the bar that particular night, the resigned reply was a reflective, "Well,... we really haven't had much business lately,...not since my husband died,...and television came in." They were both trying to hang on, in a losing battle, to what they knew and valued. I bought another round to support her memories.

So the Community Club disbanded after a short lived, and maybe not even valiant, effort. The school was sold, and torn down. Some good neighbors eventually built a house on the lot. In a sentimental gesture they preserved and positioned the school bell and its canopy on the corner of the lot as an historical remembrance for the community. And the bell was stolen.

Chapter 12
Urban Renewal

Strategic planning was not one of the trendy terms for business operations of this era, and if it had been, it never would have applied to the store. We were shaped by the schedules of delivery trucks, the weather, and farming seasons and never thought about it twice. So it was no wonder that planning to get products for the store sort of fell by default to an "as needed" (or a day after it was needed) practice.

There was generally a prepared, but ever changing, grocery list from Aunt Ruth that prompted the trek to La-Crosse for items that either had come into short supply by high demand, had been forgotten in the orders that came by truck delivery, or simply had become unavailable due to the diminishing number of wholesalers interested in the rural delivery business. This run for groceries was Uncle Alfred's job and often an impromptu invitation was offered for me to tag along. It was a natural adventure, as well as an opportunity to avoid farm chores and personally collect the latest boxes of bubble gum baseball cards from the distributors. I always began with enthusiastic inquiries of Uncle Alfred regarding departure time and the repeating reply was always "pretty quick."

I waited, and learned to cope with the emotions of boredom, frustration with being put off, guilt (minimal) from not engaging in farm chores, and anxiety that the adventure might last too long and interfere with some unknown activities and opportunities with friends that always seemed to crop up in the afternoon. Cookies and the coffee crowd were an aid in killing time, but they also delayed Uncle. The always expanding until the last minute grocery list wasn't the problem. The problem was the organization of cash and checks to deposit in the bank en route to LaCrosse, and mostly the belabored attempt to compile a list of supplies that were needed for the store, our farming operations, and the haphazard plumbing and electrical business that Uncle engaged in. Compiling a list of those materials wasn't as simple as writing down a case of beans; this list needed in depth research for the right size and quantity of fittings and specific electrical gadgetry that involved trips to the backroom, basement, and barnyard.

Approximately two and one half hours after Uncle Alfred said "pretty quick," we would embark for LaCrosse. LaCrosse is a beautiful river city 35 miles to the north of West Prairie that has the additional benefit of providing a scenic drive along the Great River Road. The allure of potential fishing sites on the Mississippi naturally preoccupied my adolescent mindset. Years later as I recreated the trip, I witnessed the early morning sun shoot its spotlight through a gap in the eastern bluffs of the river, focusing on a fog enshrouded island that was ablaze in the red, orange and brown leaves of fall. In that instant the river was forever something more spiritual and mysterious than a fishing site or route marker.

The LaCrosse riverfront warehouse district was a merger of roads, the river, railroad, and the Mississippi River Bridge from Minnesota. To the north of the deteriorating grocery warehouses, the city supported more substantial and upscale wholesale buildings that supplied contractors, plumbers and electricians. Somewhat to the south, the route by which we entered the city, the G. Heileman Brewing Company—a staple of the local economy and neighborhood taverns – sat formidably, including the six, fifty foot high, steel holding tanks painted with the *Old Style* labels and appropriately called the world's largest six-pack. To the west was the undistinguished bank of the Mississippi with run down docking facilities and crumpled concrete memories of river trade. And to the near east was Third Street, a tavern and beer haven that fueled college students and a vast array of other clientele in a milieu of bars, dance clubs and businesses that spilled over from the adjacent downtown business district. Someone in the business of urban planning likely would have predicted that these boundaries would remain intact in some fashion, and that the core, the warehouse district that had long supported the thriving commerce of bridges, roads and river, would be the one pressed to change.

With the acquisition of a driver's license, and the confidence of my elders, the grocery run to LaCrosse would occasionally become a solo venture. This exciting context of new freedoms and responsibilities served to positively rebuild and enhance the memories that had been repressed by the experience of waiting for the trip with Uncle Alfred.

Finding a place to park near the desired wholesale grocery warehouse was challenging amidst the hustle and bustle of delivery trucks, pick-up trucks and cars on cramped red brick-paved streets that paralleled the Mississippi River waterfront. The anxiety of pulling into a reserved space, or maneuvering into a gap between large delivery trucks was compounded by the fact that I was a newly licensed driver, unsure of the unwritten traffic protocols of the narrow streets and alleys. Ultimately, parking decisions came under the "anything goes as long as you don't stay there too long" rule.

The warehouses either shared common walls or they were sandwiched so close together that they could have. Names of the distributors were noted in faded paint on exterior brick walls or on the double wide, wooden and glass doors that rattled open. But the district did little else to welcome customers. Warehouses had little need or interest in marketing or fancy self promotion, so large girly or sporting scene calendars frequently served as the sole décor of the dark and dingy interiors that were lit by suspended bare light bulbs or unadorned commercial fixtures. Entering the rickety and inauspicious front doors that were usually propped open, one stared at seemingly endless rows of multi-story shelving and wooden staircases that appeared to seamlessly merge with each other, and form an intricate maze that might meld the interior of our most popular distributor, Selrite Foods, into the caverns of adjacent Front Street buildings. The aisles were a veritable obstacle course, the dark and worn wood floors filled with cases of canned goods, ladders, heavy wooden carts, and a flow of warehouse workers who negotiated the maze of cardboard boxes and burlap sacks of produce.

A small counter, surrounded by boxes and dollies, and stacked with clipboards, files, and miscellaneous office supplies merged with the end of a long stacked grocery shelf to function as the central spot for retailers to place their orders. No part of the site suggested a reception area or greeting point, and usually it was void of staffing, so I would anxiously wait in this area (since there was no obvious alternative) to see if I had been noticed and actually had found the location to place our grocery order. I carefully rehearsed my opening comments, making sure I would remember to give them both operational names of the store, either the West Prairie or Allen Halverson Store. Eventually a warehouse clerk would show up, take the order from my crumpled list with barely a word, scratch it onto a multi-row checklist order form in carbon paper triplicate, and pass the clipboard to the back regions of the counter. From there I lost sight of the clerk, and my order, and again engaged in lonely waiting, hoping the order was actually being filled and not filed for truck delivery later in the week. When the first case of vegetables would unceremoniously arrive and, without comment, be dumped on a cart, I would begin to closely inventory my order, since there was rarely a confirmation that the entire order had officially been completed.

Progressing to the plumbing and electrical ware-houses, the process was more defined. Real parking spaces fronted the buildings, and brightly lit showrooms and reception counters with full time clerks served to entertain and focus the visit. I knew canned vegetables and potato sacks, but if there was any doubt regarding the description of the plumbing and electrical supplies, I was totally help-less, and at the mercy of well-intended stock clerks. The pre cell phone era resulted in returned merchandise and more careful planning for the next trip.

Eventually the grocery warehouse district was gone, perhaps the only tangible memory being a few attempts to retain some brick walkways. The area was consciously transformed to a hotel, convention, shopping and dining district, that overlooked a luxurious river park. And the limited groceries that lined the West Prairie shelves (three boxes positioned sideways to occupy space, rather than a stacked high case) often came from a much different form of merchandise acquisition – shopping runs to the big grocery *retailers* in Iowa or LaCrosse, in search of advertised spe-cials. A quarter mark-up in the price would feel like profit, without consideration given to the overhead costs of travel and gasoline. By this time, any effort to stock our shelves was business self-deception. It was a dying operation that grasped at any measure to preserve a community center that had a symbiotic relationship between operators and customers. And maybe the shopping run would include the search for a box of the favorite cereal for the farmer's wife who lived just down the road. I like to think that maybe, just maybe, she had picked that particular box off the big city shelf herself earlier in the week, only to reflectively put in back in place, knowing it was one of the few items she could still find in West Prairie.

As the decades progressed, the whisper of Wal-Mart crept through business and shopping conversations, and even in the store, there was a hint that Wal-Mart was the nemesis that sucked the lifeblood from country retailers. But it wasn't Wal-Mart that killed us. It was our lack of business organization and inability to plan, adapt and foresee the need for convenience stores (that sold coffee instead of giving it away); and, of course, the lack of a wholesale distribution system that had suffered death by the phenomenon known as urban renewal.

Chapter 13
Redwing Blackbirds

In the late spring, when the roadway ditches and banks were beginning to fill with new growth grasses, weeds and brush that were starting to smother the dry brown remains from the previous year, there was one species that fully claimed this province as their own – the redwing blackbird. Walking the rural byways at that time of year subjected the walker to incessant swooping, dive-bombing and menacing squawks, as the inhabitants attempted to ward off intruders from their nesting areas. Even more intimidating than walking, and potentially treacherous, was following one's natural instinct to swerve a bicycle to avoid the persistent attacks. I often elected to walk. Still, their dives consistently came within two feet of the passersby, but never made contact.

The North West Prairie Church was only half a mile from the store, but it was a busy highway and a segment of it was well guarded by the redwings as we made the bicycle trip to Vacation Bible School. Whoever dreamed up that name for biblical and religious education that began within one week of the public school summer closing should have been employed as political advisor engaged in writing the script for double-speak addresses. Instead of that enticing misnomer, truth in advertising would have called it "Vacation Delaying Bible School." Dodging the birds made it seem a double insult, just when we were looking forward to summer.

And it wasn't a great time of year for the farming community to keep the kids from working in the fields of ripe hay and plowed tobacco fields ready for planting. I truly believe that the mothers and the high school girls from the community, who were enlisted to teach, were committed to what they were doing in Bible School, but it was also likely that their arms had been twisted. And maybe it was just me (I wouldn't bet on it), but when it came to the "should go" of Bible School, the "should" felt a lot less spiritually motivated than it did on Sunday mornings.

Of course the idea was to make it fun but I have never been particularly artistic or an enthusiastic experiential learner, so the crafted arks and crosses did little for my spiritual development. We even played some softball, but it was supposed to be fun. Everyone was included, and we had to be nice. It lacked the thrill of dust and competition that we lived for in the regular school yard. And since I didn't sing well or know anything about music, putting all sorts of motions and hand signals into the group singing events didn't do much for me either. In fact, it got me into trouble.

It was probably related to the difficulty of annually enticing teachers for Bible School that one year we had an itinerant preacher assume leadership. Most of us, even at that young age, related to this church strategy as something that pushed us toward rebellion.

The fateful setting was the third row of church pews, right side of the aisle, just in front of the pulpit. The smaller kids were in the pews left of the main aisle. We had disbanded from our small class groups, and congregated for large group singing in the front pews of the church. The song was the ever popular *Deep and Wide*. The hand gestures to the title line called for one hand raised high above the head, with the other stretched low beneath one's waist. It was quickly followed by wide spread arms that combined with the first gesture to signify how deep and wide was the grace flowing from the fountain of God's love. The second set of gestures mimicked a fountain, hands clasped at the waist and rising to eye level, then sweeping apart in dramatic fashion indicating the spreading nature of God's mercy. It might have been fun, and with some fortune even engaged some symbolic learning if we had made it as far as the second set of gestures. We didn't.

We didn't get in *deep* trouble; rather it was *wide* trouble when that part of the gestures set the preacher off, as my friends and I enthusiastically swept each other several feet to left and right in the pew. Apparently it wasn't as funny as we thought. The resulting less than merciful response on the preacher's part was to parade us up in front of the altar to share our musical and gesturing talents with the entire Bible School. More than forty years later, I am hard pressed to remember any other tangible experience from Bible School.

Sometimes it wasn't easy being a kid in church, or biking with blackbirds.

The rural school didn't survive, and the country store didn't either. But, the church did. It probably comes back to the deep and wide thing, and the people who keep the fountain flowing. And the redwings are still there. I have learned not to swerve my bike. They are resilient and beautiful as they sway back and forth in the wind, clasping a thin blade of grass.

Chapter 14
Mentors at the Country Store Crossroads

I have heard lots of talk about mentoring and despite what career journals and educational institutions espouse, I mostly come to think of mentoring for me as a formative process that happened long ago. As I recall growing up in the store, I am reminded that mentoring is often a function of place. Because of its location and diverse social interchanges the store was rich in opportunities for a kid like me to bask in exposure to people who weren't traditional teachers, career builders, or premeditated good-deed-doers. Good people were just there; and, had the opportunity to be there. Reflecting deeper on that experience, I now see more clearly some of the mentoring from the crossroads.

- When I was watching the fuzzy black and white television in the back room of the store, adjusting the rabbit ears and focused on the *Saturday Game of the Week* (there was only one baseball game a week on television in those days), it was Jeanne, from a local farm, who jumped in jubilation and hugged me when the unlikely Roy Mc-

Millan hit a home run off the foul pole in the bottom of the 9th to win the game. I now deeply suspect she didn't give a rip about the Cincinnati Reds.

- It was Sonny, the traveling dry-cleaner representative, whose warm smile and friendly conversation was always a blessing late in the afternoon when most store traffic had subsided. He was soft and gentle to all. But it was clearly going the extra mile when he would show up unexpectedly at one of my out of town high school basketball games, surprising both me and my parents in a locale that was far away from our comfort zones.

- It was Butch, the Sunbeam bread delivery-man (none of those guys had real names), who would drink gallons of coffee each week and philosophize over the coffee table with local farmers and other salesmen. During a deep conversation on the topic of the kids going to hell in a hand basket because the boys were now wearing long hair, a local tough guy parent said that no son of his would ever sit at *his* table with long hair. Butch, the philosopher, knowing the broader impact of such rigid parenting, was overheard to say, "No, you're right, Joe, he probably won't."

- It was the Norwegian bachelor farmer Johnnie, whose fishing stories were well known throughout the county to be exaggerated by at least 40%. But he took me fishing. It was during one such trip, in the middle of a thunderous rain and hail storm, which kept us (especially me) terrified, sitting in his push-button-shift purple Dodge, rather than on the banks of the Mississippi, when he calmly said that we would just have to do what they did in Norway on such occasions. I bit on that line like a hungry fish and said, "What's that?" He chuckled and said, "They let it rain."

- My mother's vegetable garden, Uncle Alfred's infamous and obsessively plotted dahlia bed, and Aunt Ruth's grape vines and raspberry bushes – all provided work and mentoring experiences that perhaps were not fully appreciated at the time. But in both the literal and figurative sense they were seeds, visions, and transplants for the future.

- It was Bernice whose voice twinkled as she called me by name, communicating with that and her following inquiries that she was always interested in my life.

- Before OSHA and other regulations filtered into retail operations, Uncle Alfred and Aunt Ruth mentored an adolescent in the judicious use of meat slicers and gas pumps. Whether or not this communicated good judgment, it certainly communicated trust.

- An array of tolerant customers believed in me and patiently witnessed me hone my penmanship and math skills on their daily grocery tabs. They somehow figured out what else was happening in my world as they waited.

- And it was a local, aged preacher, Pastor Nords-letten, who would stop at our country story for a friendly cup of coffee and what he called some of that "good West Prairie gas" on his way to friends in Osage, Iowa. But he also made it clear, every time, that I was absolutely the best person in the world to pump that gas.

Some of it came full circle. Bernice got a draft copy of this book before she died. Her voice still twinkled. The old bachelor farmer Johnnie "moved to town," as old bachelor farmers are wont to do as they age and can no longer cope with the driveway mud or accumulated snow. But he made my visit list when I made an infrequent return to "the prairie." Many of the extra "mothers" I had in the store found their way to my first book signing and got a well deserved hug, and passed their stories of community on to their children and grandchildren. When it doesn't come full circle, sometimes the opportunities for tangents grace our lives. Maybe that church garden that I tilled years later caught one or two of the long hidden seeds that had crept into the cuffs of my blue jeans, and maybe, just maybe, they found rich soil where some kid shared their hopes and fears as they weeded a patch of beans.

Chapter 15
Life above the Store

While the sturdy structure that has rattled, swayed and withstood strong winds for over 100 years was always a community landmark, it was never well maintained during my lifetime. Perhaps, once during my residence I recall the short term satisfaction that accompanied a fresh coat of gray paint with red trim. But the wood frame building and siding was so dry that the freshness was short-lived. I identify with the store as a run-down structure (side by side with our used 1953 gray Plymouth that looked just about as dilapidated) that an embarrassed teen-ager would painstakingly keep from the view of all but his closest friends. There were redeeming characteristics such as the small stained glass squares that surrounded the huge glass front windows, but their character was diminished by the bare siding and rickety front screen door that bore the faded Sunbeam Bread push-bar and door handle.

Fortunately the paint hungry building served well as my playground. The "back room" on the east side of the store, used mostly as storage, appeared as a covered lean-to type structure and appendage to the box and pitched roof store architecture. On occasion when my brother and I managed to open a clear row between cases of groceries, we would strap metal skates onto our shoes, and traverse the aisles, taking care to avoid sharp table edges or crashes that might disrupt the kerosene pump in the far corner of the room. Inside play had its natural limitations, but outside gave way to imagination.

The ten foot high exterior east wall was topped by a slanted tin roof that climbed to the second floor porch and entry way for our apartment. It also functioned as the deep left field wall for the baseball field that fed my solo baseball fantasies for hours on end, that crept into full summers, before my age eventually transported me to city baseball diamonds and high school teams. From the far corner of the store yard, I fantasized being Hank Aaron as the Milwaukee Braves trailed by three runs in the bottom of the 9th. Momentarily, after I tossed the baseball in the air, my posture and grip on the bat was transformed into the classic Aaron stance, arms outstretched, with bat pointing directly skyward – and then in an instant, a quick wrist driven swing would scream a line drive deep to left center and the ball would land on the tin roof, as the Milwaukee County Stadium fans erupted in cheers, elated over the grand slam heroics of their, and my, hero. The ritual repeated itself with lesser heroes such as Adcock, Pafko, Burdette, or Crandall. And the lefties of Covington, Mathews; or even the pitcher, Spahn, would occasionally drift a fly ball high enough to clear my mother's right field flower garden, land on the blacktop of Highway 82, and bounce across to the neighbor's tobacco field to win yet another game.

While life in and about the store afforded some creative and sometimes unusual recreation, other aspects of growing up in the store presented even more unique experiences that melded business, personal life, and community intersections into a package that shaped the way I have viewed and related to the world.

At the simplest level, life in the store warped my perspective of grocery shopping. It was something *other* people did. My shopping involved running up and down the stairs to the store several times a day when my mother began meal preparation. There was never a grocery bag or significant list of items to purchase, although on occasion some canned goods might escape overloaded arms and tumble back down the long staircase. Bread was always fresh, but sometimes arrived mangled when it temporarily took on the life of a football during the trip upstairs. I knew that practice had finally reached its limits, when my father suggested sarcastically that in contrast to the advertising jingle "Soft, Fresh, Tenderly Twisted, Sunbeam Tender Twist Bread," the bread just delivered to his table had been "viciously squeezed."

My current encounters with grocery stores provoke an inordinate desire to price shop and then overstock my cupboards, undoubtedly fueled by my training to identify bargain retail for resale in the country store. I always stand in wonder at the variety that we now love, but never really needed in the country. I don't buy what I might need to cook a normal meal, subconsciously thinking the needed items will magically appear from the store beneath my kitchen. And when I encounter the small corner grocery, a mom and pop operation, or country store, I always buy something whether it is needed or not.

The upstairs life was also privy to the world below, either visually as we watched the customer traffic and selectively decided whom we might go down to visit, or audibly because the thin wood floors transferred the emotional messages from below, if not the words themselves. And some of those sounds would predict Aunt Ruth's journey upstairs for respite from family arguments, or the burdens left by friends at the coffee table. And sometimes the phone would ring to announce that someone headed up the staircase needed more consolation and privacy than the downstairs public coffee table could provide.

Ultimately, as I reflect on my own world and how I relate to people, the influence of living in and experiencing the store becomes obvious. There were lessons learned. On the down side, I never have been a successful entrepreneur or particularly skilled at planning for business-like ventures. The history emulated is that of a marginal retailing enterprise with other agendas (perhaps fuzzy and subconscious), currently exhibited by West Prairie flashbacks every time I set up shop for a garage sale, sit back in a lawn chair with a cup of coffee and seek the conversation as much as the sale. When successes have come in my life, it is often because I have simply been there for somebody. I have learned that when I am observant, with an open ear, and exhibit some minimal hospitality, enriching encounters and opportunities are inevitable. Sometimes, most of what you have to offer is just being there. The store was always there, unkempt and unprofitable, but stable and welcoming.

Beyond the symbiotic and intimate relationship with store life, the penthouse was an observation point for the highway (milk-trucks, ambulances, farm machinery, store customers, bicyclists and kids returning from school). It also afforded an inconspicuous and quiet watchtower and place of reflection, as my mother waited for her teenage boys who had been out late at night. Would they come back safely; had they been good? In the daylight hours, perhaps she saw me driving and skidding the red Farmall Model A tractor in the fields as I learned to compensate for slides in the mud and snow, thinking that would make me a better driver when I was old enough to get a license; and then she glimpsed in the other direction to see cars cruising down the highway, past and through the crossroads. And maybe she pondered why nobody taught her to skillfully drive a farm tractor, and what ultimately kept her from getting a driver's license, and how her life might have been different had she experienced the freedom of the road. And what if her father had encouraged attending business college, rather than pose that question years later, expressing his surprise that she had not gone? Might she have run a successful business somewhere else, rather than be the silent glue that gently bound together and supported this place at the crossroads?

I know the questions were there, but her innermost reflections have never surfaced. Perhaps the lost opportunities are only conjecture or projection on my part. I prefer to think that she experienced a quiet peace with her role in the penthouse and store community as she reflectively looked out the window and viewed the barns, crops, farm animals, and our family as we collectively traversed the farm pathways. Her favorite images from the south facing kitchen windows were those of my father, my brother and me, laughing as we walked from barn to shed, to field, perhaps recreating an image and song from the corny humor of the popular *Hee Haw* television show. Those family treks often involved meandering down County Highway N, which served as the dividing line between our two farms. The road – as a marker, a means of access, exit, or opportunity – was always there.

For me the ingrained images and meaning conjured up by the highway incorporate and, in an embracing way, stretch beyond our family relationships, as shared with the West Prairie community in my father's funeral eulogy:

> *It was time for him to go, and I certainly appreciate, as would Lee, the fact that he died peacefully on the Sabbath, a day he always honored, and a day of rest, made even more appropriate by the fact that it was a wonderful rainy weekend, as Lee would have said, "it was a million dollar rain."*

> *I was struck in church this morning, coincidentally (or not) about the same time Lee died, as the rain, the million dollar rain, came down, visible through our church windows, that the sermon was all about hospitality. That is certainly what Lee was all about, no better exhibited than by his multiple forms of deep hospitality to the many friends, wayward souls, salesmen, travelers, family members and other sojourners that made their way to the crossroads of County Trunk N and Highway 82.*

When last fall, Lee had apparently suffered a stroke, and many of us thought his death was imminent, I inquired how he was doing. He said that maybe others didn't think he was doing so well, but he gratefully said, "You know, I haven't had a bad day in my life." What a blessing, and what a way to gracefully leave this world.

One of his favorite jokes was to saunter down County Trunk N, carrying an old suitcase (filled with tools, not traveling clothes), singing the words from a famous Merle Haggard country song, "Down Every Road There's Always One More City." I think he just got there.

The community grieved his loss in the summer of 2005, and revisited the grief of a country store that Lee, Helen and Aunt Ruth had closed eight years earlier – a community fixture that shared his open hospitality. And so the rest of us are left to look down the road for the next city, the sojourners in our paths, and the opportunities of our own crossroads.

The Crossroads - County N and Hwy 82

Chapter 16
Epilogue—Aunt Ruth

Since the original completion of this book the abandoned store was sold for a private residence. My mother continued to live in the farmhouse across the road with my brother Dave and his wife, Toni. They eventually moved; and Aunt Ruth died at the age of 95.

I guess her timing was good. It would have seemed a bit much to end a book with two funeral stories. She wouldn't have laughed at a remark like that about the timing of her funeral, but instead would have gathered up half a smile on one side of her mouth and lifted one eyebrow, indicative of questioning, but loving, approval.

Funeral home visitations have gradually attempted to replace mournful atmospheres with the emphasis on celebrations of life. With Aunt Ruth's age, a productive and appreciated life, and the relief that accompanies death after a long illness that had diminished almost any quality of life she had, the atmosphere was relaxed, informal and yes, celebratory. Modern technology provided for gathering at one corner of the funeral home where a DVD played gentle music while displaying 50 pictures that scanned Ruth's lifespan. Friends and family were pleased to see themselves and recall moments that had slipped from their memories. Surprises such as the candid photo of Ruth confidently striding down a busy and windy Chicago street, left the viewer questioning why this potential fashion model left the big city to return to a ragged and unprofitable country store.

During the visitation and funeral more stories emerged. A member of the Saturday morning group that gathered around the store coffee table to cut hair and give permanents shared Ruth's quiet and accepting ways, noting Ruth's gentle comment about a mild headache hours later because the hair rollers had been set too tight. A visitor who barely knew Ruth was there because her spouse had experienced uncommon hospitality as he passed through West Prairie. Others recalled her baking skills, long standing contributions to running the county fair, and work as a Sunday School teacher and superintendent.

Ruth might have conjured up a chuckle if she knew about the television and VCR that played only 20 feet away from her pink trimmed casket that was adorned with pink flowers and a frumpled old toy kitty that had kept her company in the recent years of nursing home residency. A former neighbor had videotaped the 100th anniversary of the store and that hour long tape played continuously during the visitation. I wonder what Ruth would have thought about that activity replacing the standard prayer service and scripture reading. Initially, I too wondered about the appropriateness of the taped intrusion that seemed to invade the solemn casket corner.

But as I watched her friends and former community members view the tape, laugh and reminisce, it became clear that Ruth's identity and the rich community built around the store were synonymous. This was not an invasion of her space. She would not have viewed it that way. The funeral home dance was a gentle revelation that as the rest of the gathering was laughing in fellowship or sharing a memory, Ruth was once again in the quiet and unassuming background role that she lived within the store. She was building community.

***

3018632

Made in the USA